JANUARY BIBLE STUDY

God's Amazing Grace

Studies in Romans

Written by
Dean Register

LifeWay Press®
Nashville, TN

ISBN: 1-4158-3227-7
Item: 005035374

This book is a resource in the Leadership and Skill Development category of the Christian Growth Study Plan.
Course CG-1176

Subject Area: Bible Studies
Dewey Decimal Classification Number: 234.1
Subject Heading: GRACE (THEOLOGY) \ BIBLE. N.T. ROMANS-STUDY \ SALVATION

Printed in the United States of America

Leadership and Adult Publishing
LifeWay Church Resources
One LifeWay Plaza
Nashville, TN 37234-0175

We believe the Bible has God for its author; salvation for its end; and truth, without any mixture of error, for its matter and that all Scripture is totally true and trustworthy. The 2000 statement of The Baptist Faith and Message is our doctrinal guideline.

Cover Image: DesignPics

Contents

Session 1

Can I Believe in God? (Rom. 1:1–4:25)

Session 2

Is God Still Active Today? (Rom. 5:1–7:25)

Session 3

Does God Care About Me? (Rom. 8:1–11:36)

Session 4

Does God Care How I Live? (Rom. 12:1–16:27)

From the Editor

BECAUSE OF HIS AMAZING GRACE, God gives salvation to those who respond with faith in Jesus. Further, He helps them to meet His expectations of living transformed lives. This study in Romans is designed to lead adults to acknowledge that the grace of God is the basis of salvation and to agree that those who receive this salvation are to meet His expectations of transformed living. In his **Letter to the Romans,** Paul centered on four questions that are still relevant today: Can I believe in God? Is God still active today? Does God care about me? Does God care how I live? These questions provide the outline for this **January Bible Study 2008.**

This **Learner Guide** is written in an informal, easy-to-read style that helps the reader understand the biblical text without extensive comments. It also has a series of helps to enhance each reader's study. These helps include:

- **Learning activities** in each chapter. Each activity is integral to the teaching plans in the Leader Guide.
- A least one feature entitled **A Closer Look** in each chapter that elaborates on or provides summary information on related chapter topics.
- Sets of questions entitled **For Your Consideration** occur throughout each chapter. Some questions relate to Bible content. Some are application questions that help learners focus on the passage's present-day meaning for their lives. These questions can be used in individual or group study, and with the Learning Activities can help a group leader stimulate discussion.

At the beginning of each lesson you will find the **Bible Truth** and **Life Impact.** The **Bible Truth** briefly states the main abiding spiritual principle for that lesson. The **Life Impact** identifies how learners will give evidence of spiritual transformation on an ongoing basis. This is the main application we hope learners will take with them after the session is over.

Dr. Dean Register wrote this Learner Guide. Dr. Register is the senior pastor at Temple Baptist Church, Hattiesburg, Mississippi. Dr. Register is a graduate of Valdosta State University (B.A.); New Orleans Baptist Theological Seminary (M.Div., Th.D.); and Reformed Theological Seminary (Th.M.). He did additional study at Oxford University, Oxford, England.

God Reveals Himself

Introduction (Rom. 1:1-4)

When Tom and I first met, we connected quickly and became friends. We both enjoyed many of the same activities, such as spending time with our families, playing sports, going on adventures, and engaging in a good debate on occasion. Tom didn't like God, however. He doubted God's existence and often quizzed me with sharp questions like: How can I believe in God when suffering is so rampant? Isn't faith in God a mere projection of an inner longing? Why should I trust Him when He won't reveal Himself?

Tom's questions are common. Clearly, one of the most important issues we face is "How can we believe in God when we live in a culture of doubt and unbelief?" Relativism contends that there is no absolute truth about God since all truth is relative to personal preference. Darwinism claims that there is no rationale for belief in God because the universe

BIBLE TRUTH:
We can be sure God exists because He reveals Himself to us.

LIFE IMPACT:
To help you have confidence about your belief in God

Interior of the prison in Rome where tradition says Paul was held prior to his execution.

developed randomly without a designer. Pluralism argues that the God revealed in Scripture is too exclusive since all gods are equally true.

Belief in the God of the Bible is not without controversy. If Internet search engines offer a glimpse of personal interests and values, each day in America approximately 32 million searches are made for the term "sex" while less than 1-1/2 million are for the term "god" (*SBC Life* June-July, 2002). Statistics show that the majority of American adults don't believe absolute truth exists. Should we think it strange that millions refuse to embrace the God of Scripture when the table of deception and the couch of pleasure are so prominent in our culture?

In the first-century city of Rome, Christians lived in a similar context. The city teemed with moral uncertainty, religious idolatry, and social diversity. Into such an environment Paul presented the realty of the one and only God and the life-changing truth of God's amazing grace.

Paul identified himself as a "slave of Christ Jesus" (v. 1). Although no urbane Roman would embrace the title of "slave," Paul willingly chose it as a badge of honor. He saw himself as being owned by Christ. His identity was centered in a relationship of total devotion to his Savior. Paul never lost the wonder of grace bestowed so freely upon him by Christ. Consequently, he viewed his entire life under the claim of his Master.

For Your Consideration

How would you describe your relationship to Christ right now?

_____

_____

_____

_____

Paul further described himself as an "apostle" who was "singled out" for a redemptive mission. He knew the mission was not an assignment he created, but a calling from God he could not avoid. God appointed him as an authorized messenger to testify about the gospel. God commissioned him to communicate the good news of salvation promised by the "prophets" and rooted in "the Holy Scriptures" (v. 2). Paul stood upon the reliability of the Old Testament and the messianic prophesies to proclaim the truth concerning Jesus.

Notice the balanced way Paul emphasized both the humanity and deity of Jesus. The phrase "a descendant of David according to the flesh" (v. 3) underscored the human nature of the Son of God. Unlike

LEARNING ACTIVITY

Authority Figures

Place a *W* in front of the three people or things that most influence what you wear. Do the same for the following: *T* for where you spend your time; *P* for your political views; *E* for your entertainment choices. Finally, circle the three persons or things that most influence what you believe about God.

___ Parents	___ Elected officials	___ Co-workers
___ Boss	___ Children	___ Newspaper
___ Friends	___ Pastor	___ Books
___ Extended Family	___ Television	___ Traditions
___ Spouse	___ Laws	___ Internet
___ Neighbors	___ Magazine	

many mythological deities of the Romans, Jesus was born into a real human family. He demonstrated the essence of humanness in perfection and never sinned. He ate when He was hungry. He sweated when He was hot. He rested when He was tired. He bled when He was crucified. Through the human lineage of David, Jesus fulfilled the holy promise of a Kingdom that would reign eternally. (See Isa. 9:7; Jer. 23:5.)

The phrase "established as the powerful Son of God by the resurrection" (v. 4) expressed the divine nature of Jesus. The resurrection validated His deity. It didn't make Him the Son of God, but it proved He had been the Son of God eternally. If Jesus was only human and not also divine then He was blasphemous to God. If He was only divine and not also human He was irrelevant to humanity. The Bible affirms that Jesus was both fully human and fully God. We can trust Him in life and for eternity because He conquered sin on the cross and death by the resurrection. Christianity stands on the resurrection as a life-changing event. Paul didn't say to the Romans, *Listen to what I feel about Jesus.* He said, *Listen to this event about the resurrection of Jesus.* The event was a supernatural accomplishment by "the Spirit of holiness" (v. 4), also known as the Holy Spirit. We can believe the event to be true for two reasons: reliable eyewitness testimony and changed lives.

My dad was an Army sergeant during World War II. When the Germans surrendered to the American and Allied forces to end the war, I wasn't present, but I believe the event happened for two reasons. First, I believe the testimony of those who were present. I have examined their story and found it to be credible and authentic. Second, I believe it occurred because had Hitler and the German army not been defeated, the world would have been vastly different under the rule of Nazi oppression.

Obviously, I wasn't present to verify the resurrection either. I believe it happened because of evidence from the eyewitnesses who testified about it. Jesus appeared to the disciples, to several individuals, and to 500 others. Another reason I believe is because of the change the resurrection made in the lives of the early Christians then and in the lives of believers today. Had Jesus lost to death and the resurrection had been a mere dream, the world would be a vastly different place. There would be no Christian faith or church. There would be no hope of eternal life. Despair would dominate and death would reign.

Believe in God: He Reveals His Righteousness (Rom. 1:14-17)

A fundamental fact of the gospel is that we are not able to save ourselves from the penalty of sin and death. Only God can break the grip of sin and set us free from death's captivity. Consequently, the gospel reveals God's righteousness against the backdrop of our depravity.

11

Paul was consumed by a desire to communicate three truths regarding the relevance of God's righteousness. First, he expressed an obligation to the recipients of the gospel. Paul believed that the good news of God's gracious salvation was a message he was compelled to share with the "Greeks and barbarians" and with the "wise and the foolish" (v. 14). Essentially, Paul affirmed his duty to take the message to anyone and everyone regardless of education, sophistication, vocation, or nationality.

For Your Consideration
1. In what way do you identify with Paul's obligation? Do you feel a similar desire to share the gospel?

---

2. What would be the identifying characteristics of a person whose top priority was the spread of the gospel?

Paul would not consider keeping the gospel to himself, and he could not remain silent. God expects believers to tell unbelievers that He has revealed His righteousness in Christ. God is pleased when His followers tell others how to follow His Son.

Millions of people die each year from cancer. Suppose you were a medical scientist and you discovered a cure for cancer. Could you entertain the thought of keeping the cure to yourself? Wouldn't you embrace an obligation to offer every willing person the life-sustaining medicine?

Second, Paul expressed his eagerness to preach the gospel. The word "eager" (v. 15) refers to a passionate desire. The word "preach" in this context refers to an announcement of the gospel. Paul was excited, ready, and zealously anticipating the opportunity of witnessing in Rome. He could hardly wait to

LEARNING ACTIVITY

Confidence Scale

On a scale of 1 to 10 (with 1 being the lowest), rate your level of confidence in believing God exists and how He reveals Himself to you.

I have confidence about believing in God because:

1	2	3	4	5	6	7	8	9	10

He reveals His righteousness

1	2	3	4	5	6	7	8	9	10

He reveals His wrath

1	2	3	4	5	6	7	8	9	10

He reveals His attributes

1	2	3	4	5	6	7	8	9	10

He reveals His expectations

declare the only answer to humanity's deepest problem in a city proud of its own sufficiency. The eagerness factor challenges us to be ready to tell our story of conversion. Like Paul, we want to faithfully articulate the change Jesus made in our lives by announcing God's amazing grace.

Third, Paul expressed his bold confidence in the gospel. The Greek word for "ashamed" (v. 16) describes feelings related to something of a dubious nature. Nothing about the gospel caused Paul to feel shame. The gospel had never been the source of any disappointment. Consequently, he had never lost confidence in the gospel's transforming capacity. The sustaining reason for

Paul's bold confidence lay in his conviction about the gospel as "God's power for salvation" (v. 16). To say that the gospel is "God's power" is to affirm the authority and activity of God in the message of His righteous redemption. His transforming reality breathes through the gospel. Much has been made over the word "power" as a derivative of the Greek word *dunamis* which is associated with our words dynamo, dynamic, and dynamite. Indeed, the gospel can blast like dynamite through the hardened layers of human pride, but the meaning reaches farther. The gospel's power is a dynamic quality of the infinite God. The gospel taps into God's omnipotence and stands completely on His strength.

Paul explained that the power of the gospel for salvation was available to all people. If that's true, then why did he say it began with the Jews? Because historically God conveyed His righteousness first through Abraham and then confirmed His redeeming purpose through the people of Israel.

Paul was convinced not only of the gospel's power, he was certain of its competence in revealing God's righteousness. He wrote "in it [the gospel] God's righteousness is revealed from faith to faith" (v. 17).

God's righteousness involves His holiness acquitting us of wrongdoing and conferring on us a new status. Faith is essential in this experience, but it is not a meritorious action. Through faith we receive God's righteousness. Consequently, faith is a necessary response for the salvation event and also a crucial component for Christian living.

Believe in God: He Reveals His Wrath
(Rom. 1:18,21-27)

The concept of God's wrath offends many people because they think it is incompatible with God's love. Paul emphasized God's wrath to show that God's love is not neutral or passive about sin. God's wrath is His holy hostility toward "godlessness and unrighteousness" (v. 18) and His judgment on both. We should not confuse God's wrath with uncontrolled rage. His wrath is a settled virtue of His holiness rather than a random eruption of His fury.

God's wrath reacts against intentional rebellion. Don't rush past the impact of this statement: "For though they knew God, they did not glorify Him as God" (v. 21). The core problem of the human race is the

A CLOSER LOOK

Idolatry

Ironically, unbelief in the one true God is marked by belief in man-made substitutes for God. Idolatry is alive and flourishing in our culture just as it was in the Roman Empire. Our idols take different forms. Instead of disfigured creatures carved in stone, our culture bows to money, sex, power, and popularity. We even produce TV programs to highlight idolatry. The word for *idol* or image (1:23) comes from a Greek word for "icon." The icons and idols of our times are pathetic attempts to substitute our desires for God's glory.

deliberate and intentional attempt to exalt self rather than honor and worship God. Unbelief is a problem arising not from the absence of God's revelation, but from the presence of willful reprobation. We glorify God when we acknowledge our sinfulness in light of His righteousness and give Him the adoration He is due.

In addition to God's wrath being aimed at intentional rebellion, Paul pointed out that it also targeted degrading passions. Once perversity lodges in the mind, it spreads quickly and becomes a lifestyle. Deluded thinking leads to degenerate behavior.

For Your Consideration

1. Do you think idolatry in our society is more pronounced now compared to a generation ago? If so, in what ways?

_____

_____

2. What contemporary idols are most tempting to you?

_____

_____

Paul declared that people cannot spurn God without incurring His chastisement. The phrase "God delivered them over" (vv. 24,26,28) is full of present and future judgment. As a demonstration of His wrath, God removes the restraint so that the intentional rebellion and degrading passions are allowed to produce the inevitable fruit of destruction. Despite the rhetoric of the homosexual movement, God clearly condemns the practice of same-sex unions. (See vv. 26-27.) God ordained sex as a gift between a man and a woman in the covenant of marriage. Heterosexual promiscuity violates God's purpose for sex. Homosexuality likewise violates God's purpose for sex, but even worse it distorts God's design for gender.

Believe in God: He Reveals His Attributes (Rom. 1:19-20)

Paul explained that God provides evidence of himself to all human beings. God took the initiative to reveal himself through the design of creation. The evidence points to a source and the design points to a Designer. Obviously, it would be impossible for a finite person to know about the infinite God unless God decided to make Himself known.

Paul contended that God's attributes can be seen in His creation. "The heavens declare the glory of God," wrote the psalmist, "and the sky proclaims the work of His hands" (Ps. 19:1).

When I look at Mount Rushmore and see the carved faces of Washington, Jefferson, Roosevelt, and Lincoln, I don't wonder what haphazard arrangement of wind and hailstones caused that 500-foot display. Logically, I marvel at the dexterity and tenacity of the architect. Similarly, when I stare into the face of a newborn child, hike a mountain trail, or consider our globe spinning at 1,000 mph at the equator and orbiting the sun at more than 60,000 mph, I marvel at the Architect of the Universe. God gives us a glimpse of Himself in the works of His hands.

According to verse 20, the invisible attributes of God have been seen clearly since the world began. God has revealed His attributes of "eternal power" and "divine nature" in such a way that all people are accountable to Him and no one can plead ignorance or innocence.

Believe in God: He Reveals His Expectations (Rom. 2:1-16)

What does God demand of us? Because He is holy, His expectations are unwavering toward those who applaud morality as well as those who approve immorality. No person can stand on a platform of spiritual superiority. One of the ironies of human nature is our tendency to condemn others and simultaneously excuse ourselves.

God sees the entire picture. He knows our hidden agendas. He discerns our selfish motives. God's evaluation doesn't allow a comparison pitting one person against another. The standard is not another human being. The standard is God Himself. He reveals His expectations through His divine law and He makes an assessment that is inescapable and impartial.

Focus on the words "without excuse" (v. 1). What goes through your mind when you try to justify your sin? God's standard allows no exceptions because it is always "based on the truth" (v. 2). Nobody gets off the hook. Nobody can plead the Fifth Amendment in the court of God. If someone breaks a federal law there is a possibility that the person might not be apprehended, tried, convicted, or sentenced. The law-breaker could slip through the hands of human justice and live undetected for years. God's justice, however, never fails. Whoever breaks His law does not skip bail and run free. The question, "Do you really think … that you will escape God's judgment?" (v. 3), reinforces the absolute certainty that no one can avoid it.

Taken out of context, verses 9-10 might imply salvation by works. To the contrary, the central emphasis is not salvation, but God's judgment. The passage does not teach salvation by works, but judgment of our works. Therefore, God's expectation is not only inescapable, it is also impartial. He never shows partiality or "favoritism" (v. 11). Religious moralists and non-religious hedonists are weighted in the balance according to their conduct against an absolute and perfect standard.

But suppose someone should argue, "I didn't know what God expected because I didn't grow up in a religious system like Judaism." Is that a legitimate defense before the Holy Judge? Of course not. The argument is flawed because God has provided a witness in our conscience. Although our conscience can never be a perfect guide, it does function as an indicator of God's expectations. Consequently, by our conduct and our conscience we are universally accountable to the awesome God who reveals Himself.

God Accepts Our Faith

Our Need for Faith (Rom. 3:21-23)

Remember my friend Tom? The happy cynic who peppered me with hard questions about belief in God? Tom reached a turning point one day when he realized intellectual answers alone would never satisfy him. Clever arguments couldn't fill the void in his life. The hammer of his suspicion began to shatter against the anvil of God's love. Somewhat reluctantly, Tom decided to place his faith in a Savior he had never known to gain a relationship he had never experienced. A tiny step of faith made an eternal difference.

In Romans 3 Paul responded to those who object to the charge of alienation from God. He concluded that all people, whether Jew or Gentile, are under the power of sin. (See v. 9.) The whole world is alienated from God. Citing several Old Testament references, Paul pointed to the universality of sin that infects the speech and conduct of everyone. The last Old Testament refer-

BIBLE TRUTH:
We can be sure we are right with God because He accepts our faith.

LIFE IMPACT:
To help you exercise faith in God

LEARNING ACTIVITY

All Roads Lead to Rome

You're heard the phrase "All roads lead to Rome." The Romans certainly built a tremendous road system that allowed persons to travel across the Roman Empire. Use the following passages from Paul's words to the church in Rome to discover another highway system that leads to a relationship with God through Jesus Christ.

Consider sharing this road through the book of Romans with others so they can be right with God because He wants to accept their faith in Him, too.

Romans 3:23
Everyone needs to respond to God in faith because we are all sinners in need of God's grace.

Romans 5:8
God gave us a way to be saved from our sins through the death of His Son, Jesus Christ.

Romans 6:23
The payment for our sins is death, but God's grace allows us to accept His gift of eternal life if we accept Jesus as our Lord and Savior and repent of our sins.

Romans 10:9-10
Confess that Jesus Christ is Lord and believe in your heart that God raised Him from the dead and you will be saved.

Romans 10:13
Call on the name of the Lord and you will be saved.

Our faith is only as effective as its object is reliable (3:22).

ence summarizes the entire human condition. "There is no fear of God before their eyes" (v. 18). In other words, no human being, ever how pious, kind, or virtuous, can obey God sufficiently to gain entrance into heaven. The reason faith is so crucial to salvation is because the human predicament is so hopeless without Christ.

Take a moment to focus on the two little words "but now" (v. 21). They signal a transition from the peril of sin to the promise of salvation. They point to God's solution in contrast to our striving. They set the stage for the core message of Romans, namely, that God's righteousness has been revealed and it has nothing to do with our performance. It has everything to do with "faith in Jesus Christ" (v. 22). Our faith, however, is only as effective as its object is reliable. Faith in faith is worthless for salvation, but faith in God's righteousness revealed through Christ is indispensable. For example, if we walk on a frozen lake, it isn't the strength of our faith in the ice that matters. What matters is the reliability of the ice on which we stand. Consequently, faith is the means "through" which we enter a right relationship with the Lord, and the centrality of faith applies to "all who believe." Paul emphasized the need for faith by explaining that, whether Jew or Gentile, moralist or hedonist, there was "no distinction" or difference. Every person needs to place faith in Christ for salvation. We are all in the same sinking boat. We are all sipping the same poison. All of us stand on the scaffold of sin with the rope of death around our neck.

Interestingly, Paul used two verb tenses in verse 23 to illuminate our sin. "Have sinned" is an aorist tense that signifies the activity of sin in the past. "Fall short" is a present tense that signifies a continuing result of sin. We all have sinned on many occasions and we all continually fail to honor God. To "fall short" of His glory involves (1) missing His magnificent purpose for our lives, and (2) marking the spiritual distance between His righteousness and our repulsiveness. Consequently, sin is both deed and disposition. It affects our attitude and our actions. Sin is a terrorist in the soul bent on death and destruction.

For Your Consideration

1. Why is faith essential to a relationship with God?

2. In what ways do people try to earn a right standing with God apart from faith?

Our Redemption in Christ (Rom. 3:24-26)

In response to the undeniable verdict of our guilt, Paul announced the unfailing remedy of our redemption in Christ. He described redemption by using three metaphors common in Roman culture.

The first was a courtroom metaphor known as "justification." Look again at the statement "justified freely by His grace" (v. 24). Can you picture a condemned man standing before a Roman judge? The criminal is guilty and

A CLOSER LOOK

Redemption

The word "redemption" comes from a Greek word *(apolutrosis)* that occurs 10 times in the New Testament and always in connection with the saving work of Christ. Redemption was a word often heard in the slave markets of the ancient world. It denoted the liberation of a slave through the payment of a price. Paul applied it to the work of Christ and the status of lost humanity in bondage to sin. Think about it like this: Without Christ we stand in the marketplace as slaves to sin, self, and Satan. God paid our ransom, however, by the blood of His Son. He, therefore, liberated us from bondage to death. Amazingly, God served as both the originator and recipient of the ransom. What an extravagant love God displayed when, by the cross, He paid the price to release us from captivity.

deserves punishment. He awaits a stern sentence. Suddenly the judge declares a stunning reversal: "I acquit you in this court and dismiss the charges against you." Paul indicated that God's justification is given to us "freely by His grace." The term "freely" comes from a Greek word that means "without cause or cost." It reinforces the truth that God is the source of our acquittal and we cannot purchase or earn His justification. By justifying us, God put us in a right relationship with Himself and made possible our redemption.

The second metaphor is "propitiation" (v. 25) and refers to appeasement or satisfaction. Pagan belief linked propitiation to religious activity in hope of placating a bad-tempered deity. Obviously, God is not whimsical and bad-tempered. He does possess wrath, however, against sin because it opposes His righteousness. So what did Paul mean when he said, "God presented Him as propitiation"? Here's a short theological explanation. On our own merit we cannot placate the holy anger of God. So God, by His amazing love, did for us what we could never do. He satisfied His perfect holiness by the perfect offering of His sinless son on the cross. He propitiated His righteous wrath against sin without compromising His holy standard. God presented Jesus as the ultimate sacrifice to remove our guilt.

The third metaphor intersects the other two and portrays the cross as a public "demonstration." (See vv. 25-26.) The cross served as God's signal proof that whereas He had once withheld His full retribution against sin, He unleashed it all at Calvary. The phrase "passed over the sins previously committed" (v. 25) indicates God's temporary activity and merciful restraint prior to the redeeming sacrifice of Christ. The cross demonstrated that God was both the Just One and the Justifier of sinners. He satisfied the demand of His own righteousness by means of the cross and declared righteous those who put their faith in Jesus.

Our Inability to Brag
(Rom. 3:27-31)

Boasting is the universal anthem of humanity. Perhaps not obviously or loudly, but subtly, with deeply entrenched pride we vocalize our self-importance. Have you ever caught yourself embellishing a story to make yourself look better or wiser?

Paul argued that our selfish boasting has been nullified by faith. We are not able to brag about our salvation as if we accomplished it by our own merit. There is futility in thinking and behaving as if we secured our justification before God. Consequently, Paul explained that we are "justified by faith apart from works of law" (v. 28). Neither Jews, who exalt the strict details of God's commands, nor Gentiles, who pursue a different lifestyle, can coerce the hand of God. God's plan of justification provides the only foundation on which we can be accepted.

Paul anticipated a question that some of the believers would raise. The question involved the role of the moral law in regards to justification by faith. Does the practice of faith negate the moral law of God? The response "absolutely not!" represents a powerful repudiation (v. 31). A popular and similar expression today would be "no way!" Instead, faith upholds God's law. Faith provides a context for the purpose of the law. The law was designed to reveal our inability before a perfect God. The law prepared the way for salvation in Christ but it was not itself the way of salvation. Faith in Christ doesn't make us less respectful of God's law but more perceptive of God's grace. If we boast then we can boast only in "the cross of our Lord Jesus Christ" (Gal. 6:14).

For Your Consideration

In what ways can you boast about the victory Christ brings?

Our Example of Faith
(Rom. 4:1-5,13-21)

God's plan of justifying sinners by faith was not new. It could be traced all the way back to Abraham. The Jews considered Abraham to be the supreme representative of a righteous man and the father of Judaism. He, above anyone else, would have a reason to take pride in his status. He stood as a paragon of piety among men, but he had no grounds for boasting "before God" (v. 2).

If Abraham could not stand on his own morality, how did he become right with God? Three words in verse 3 answer that question and unite the old and new covenant with the practice of faith: "Abraham believed

God." (See also Gen. 15:6.) He placed his faith in God and his faith "was credited to him for righteousness" (v. 3).

Paul used an accounting analogy to explain the way God justified Abraham. First, he drew a distinction between a wage and a gift. Suppose your employer presented you with a paycheck and an attached note that read, "I wanted to give this to you out of the generosity of my heart." You looked at the check, read the note and realized it was the same amount you've been receiving every week. You would know it wasn't a gift at all. You earned it and you are entitled to it. A wage is not a gift. It's "something owed" (v. 4). You deserve it as compensation for your time, work, and knowledge. Suppose you were unable to work, however, and you received a note indicating that a wealthy donor had deposited a large check into your bank account. You would realize it was a gift and not something you earned.

Second, Paul stated that Abraham's faith was "credited for righteousness" (v. 5). The word "credited" comes from a Greek financial practice that means to impute or ascribe. It signifies a sum added to the record of someone else or ascribed to the account of another. Consequently, Abraham's faith in God was ascribed to the ledger of righteousness. His faith was "credited" by God as a gift and not something he had earned by his morality.

God's plan of justification by faith also proved true prior to the rite of circumcision. Abraham's circumcision didn't make him right with God. It only indicated the outward sign of an inward condition secured by faith. The circumcision confirmed his justification, but it did not confer a righteous status.

Paul explained that Abraham's justification was not dependent on obeying the Mosaic law because he was justified over 400 years before the law was given. The law played no role in the promise God made to Abraham. Specifically, God promised Abraham that he would be a blessing to all peoples on the earth and that Abraham would have so many descendants that he would be called "the father of many nations" (Gen. 17:5; see also 12:2.) Notice why keeping the law was insufficient for justification. First, if God's promise depended on adherence to the law then "faith is made empty" (v. 14). Second, adherence to the law produced the opposite effect of faith in God's promise. The law leads to transgression and subsequently God's wrath. Faith leads to justification and consequently God's righteousness.

LEARNING ACTIVITY

Throw Out the Lifeline

As God has thrown or is throwing the lifeline of grace to you, how are you responding? Place an X in front of the statement that most applies to you today.

____ I'm safe on the shore and see others about to drown.

____ I don't see the rope—I'm looking the other way.

____ The rope doesn't look strong, so I'll try to grab a limb or rock.

____ I want to throw the rope to others.

____ I don't think I can hold onto the rope, so I'll try to swim instead.

____ I don't trust the one throwing the rope.

____ I'm overwhelmed that someone would save me.

____ I'm too tired to hold onto a rope, so I'll take my chances floating down the river.

____ I hear the falls but I'm a good swimmer, so I'll be okay.

____ I'm encouraging others to grab hold of the rope.

____ Now that I'm safe on the shore, I don't want to go near the water again—even to help others.

For Your Consideration

1. What goes through your mind when you contemplate God's justification?

_____

_____

_____

2. In what ways do you think individuals try to "credit" themselves with righteousness?

The reason for the connection of God's promise to Abraham's faith was to reveal to Abraham's blood descendants and spiritual descendants that justification from beginning to end is "according to grace" (v. 16). The "guarantee" depends not on human achievement, but upon the graciousness of God.

Perhaps the relationship between God's grace and our faith can be clarified by an analogy. Imagine you are thrashing in the treacherous current of a rushing river. You can hear the roar of an approaching falls. The force of the water continues to pull you toward an inevitable destruction. Suddenly someone throws you a rope. You reach for it and lock your hands around it. The rescuer pulls you through the raging torrent and finally you are safe on the bank. Now we can liken this to the grace and faith connection. First, you could not have been saved unless a rope (grace) had been offered to you. Second, having been offered the rope you appropriated it by your response (faith). You were free to reject the rope, but you placed your trust in the one who tossed it to you. Did you save yourself? Of course not. The rescuer initiated your deliverance and by his action saved you from destruction when you grasped his lifeline. Grace is the Holy Rescuer offering His outrageous salvation to doomed individuals like me and you. Faith is our total dependence on Him and His plan of deliverance. When Paul said that Abraham "believed in God, who gives life to the dead and calls things into existence that do not exist" (v. 17), he was expressing the depth of Abraham's faith.

Actually, when Abraham received God's promise he was a relatively young man. By the time he realized God's promise he was a seasoned old man. He endured the years of fear and frustration. His faith faced the painful reality that he could not father a child. The expression "against hope, with hope he believed" (v. 18) underscores the tension he felt.

Abraham was 100 years old and his wife was 90. Aware of his own impotence, he trusted God's power. Realizing the "deadness of Sarah's womb" (v. 19), he believed God could make all things new. The statement that "he did not waver in unbelief" (v. 20) doesn't discount his initial laughter at the idea of bearing a son. (See Gen. 17:17.) Instead, it declares his prevailing confidence in God's ability to make possible anything considered impossible. Abraham's faith in God's promise stands as a compelling example to all believers.

Our Inclusion Through Faith
(Rom. 4:22-25)

The "therefore" that begins verse 22 marks both a conclusion regarding Abraham's example of faith and a consequence of faith that applies to all believers. Clearly, justification by faith was not limited to Abraham but has been made available to us also.

The assertion that God's offer of righteousness "was not written for Abraham alone" (v. 23) denotes a fundamental belief that Scripture is inherently relevant and infallibly reliable at all times to all peoples.

Our inclusion through faith is credited to us as righteousness when we "believe in Him who raised Jesus our Lord from the dead" (v. 24). Central to our faith is the fact of Jesus' atoning sacrifice and His resurrection from the grave. This redeeming message of God is summarized in the statement, "He was delivered up for our trespasses and raised for our justification" (v. 25). The first half of the statement looks back to the necessity of the cross as the propitiation place for our sin. The second half looks ahead and indicates that Jesus' resurrection caused our justification through faith to be a settled reality.

I have a Jewish friend who was interviewed by Larry King on CNN. Mr. King learned that he was a Christian so he asked, "Do you think Jews are going to hell?" My friend calmly replied, "I think everyone is going to hell unless they place their faith in Jesus Christ." And the good news is that Almighty God accepts our faith placed in His Son as our Savior.

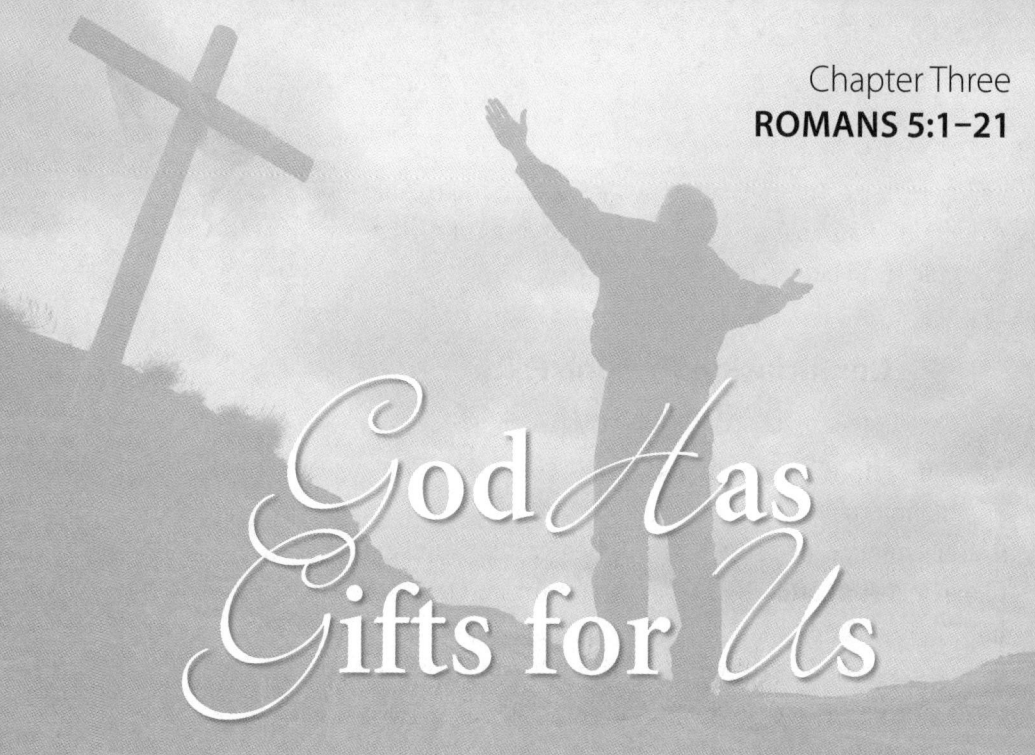

God Has Gifts for Us

BIBLE TRUTH:
We know God is active in today's world because of the gifts He offers us through Christ.

LIFE IMPACT:
To help you enjoy all the benefits of having accepted God's gifts

We Can Have God's Grace
(Rom. 5:1-5)

A business leader told me recently that he had accepted a new job. "The best part of it," he exclaimed, "is the benefit package for me and my family." Similarly, when we accept God's offer of membership into a righteous relationship, we receive by grace a benefit package that is outrageously extravagant.

"Therefore" in verse 1 shows the connection between the previous blessings of God's righteousness and the present benefits of a believer's salvation. A summary of Paul's argument in the first four chapters is succinctly linked to the statement, "since we have been declared righteous by faith" (v. 1). God's revelation of Himself (1:2–2:29) coupled with the reality of our sin and our redemption through faith (3:1–4:25) provides the theological foundation for understanding and enjoying the benefits He offers us.

LEARNING ACTIVITY

God's Gifts

Do you think God still offers us gifts today? Place an *A* (agree) in front of those with which you agree and a *D* (disagree) in front of those with which you disagree:

____ When we respond to Christ with faith, God gives us peace.

____ We can face troubles with joy, endurance, and character.

____ We can be confident about our salvation and God's activity in our lives.

____ Because of Christ's death on our behalf, we can be reconciled to God.

____ That God offers to reconcile us to Himself is all the more amazing because what He did for us in Jesus Christ was despite our being ungodly and sinners.

____ Because we all have sinned, we all need God's gift of righteousness.

____ Out of grace, God offers to make sinners righteous.

____ Because of the obedience of Jesus Christ, we can receive God's gift of eternal life.

One of the obvious benefits we experience is "peace with God" (v. 1). World peace is a noble quest, but peace among people can never be solved if peace with God is left out of the equation. Being at peace with God provides the compelling motive to seek peace with others. The word "peace" refers to a new relationship established by God for those who trust Him.

Peace is not primarily a matter of personal feelings. Instead, it is a matter of acceptance from God whereby we are no longer considered enemy combatants. Peace with God means we are no longer at war against His righteousness and we are not viewed as objects of His holy wrath.

For Your Consideration

1. How do you distinguish peace with God from the "peace of God"? (Phil. 4:7)

2. In what ways have you experienced both types of peace?

This peace is made possible through the saving work of our "Lord Jesus Christ" (v. 1). This three-fold title emphasizes the sovereignty, the humanity, and the deity of the Savior through whom "we have obtained access by faith into this grace in which we stand" (v. 2).

"Access" is another benefit we are graciously given. The Greek word for "access" denotes the act of introducing someone to royalty. The idea stirs the thought of the marvelous privilege granted to believers and reinforces the truth that we could not come to God on our own merit, but only through our Introducer—Christ Himself. Furthermore, this introduction brings us into a new position of grace "in which we stand." In ancient times a person could not simply enter the chamber of a royal monarch. An invitation was necessary. The good news is that the Sovereign God has issued us an invitation to enjoy an abiding position in His presence.

In addition to peace and access, Paul stated that we have the benefit of joyful hope, "we rejoice in the hope of the glory of God" (v. 2). Can it be possible that believers will share in the glory of God? Does that sound outrageous? The "glory of God" includes the supreme honor and renown due to God because of His perfection, as well as the brilliant radiance that always attends His presence.

Whenever we think of the word *hope,* we associate it with something we want to happen, but are not certain will. In the New Testament, hope means a confident anticipation. It emphasizes an expectation not fully realized at the present time but certain to be consummated according to God's promise.

LEARNING ACTIVITY

Benefits of Accepting God's Gifts

As you study this session, look for the benefits believers enjoy because of having accepted God's gifts. Record the benefits you found below. You may choose to underline them in your Learner Guide and/or Bible.

After the study, note the benefits you may be using more than others. Note those you may be taking for granted. Find ways to celebrate and use all of the benefits God offers believers. Share one idea with a friend or prayer partner.

By presenting the "glory of God" as the object of a believer's hope, Paul affirmed the ultimate glorification that awaits us in the perfection of our body, mind, and spirit. We should rejoice deliriously to know that God will allow us to share in His glory in heaven.

Another aspect of our joyful hope is that we are empowered to "rejoice in our afflictions" (v. 3). "Afflictions" has the meaning of "pressures." It was a word often used for squeezing olives or grapes in order to extract oil or juice. The afflictions Paul wrote about are not burdens common to everyone, but pressures and sufferings Christians face in a world hostile to the gospel. The reason we are instructed to rejoice in our afflictions is because God will use them for His glory and for our good. Instead of shielding us from suffering, the Lord uses our afflictions to produce godly qualities in us. The road of spiritual maturity invariably passes through the tunnel of tribulation. Since God develops His strongest soldiers in the valley of affliction, we can rejoice and endure the pressure knowing that He is shaping our character.

Women making olive oil. The word "afflictions" (5:3) has the meaning of "pressures" and often was used for squeezing olives or grapes in order to extract oil or juice.

A CLOSER LOOK

Original Sin

Original sin does not refer to a unique practice of sin. It is original in that its source comes through Adam and it infects the entire human race. The Bible maintains that all of us, without exception, are sinners by an inherited corruption from Adam and by personal rebellion against God. The doctrine of original sin has not always been readily embraced, however. During the 5th century a British monk named Pelagius argued against original sin and maintained that humans are not tainted by Adam's transgression. He was soundly rebuked by Augustine and Jerome, and later by the Council of Carthage in 418 A.D.

The term "proven character" (v. 4) refers to the quality in someone who has passed a test.

For Your Consideration

1. Do you find yourself being joyful only when your circumstances are pleasant?

   _____

2. When was there a time in your life that you rejoiced despite opposition toward you as a Christian?

   _____

   _____

During exam week in high school, I knew that if I studied effectively and mastered the material I didn't need to worry about a passing grade. I didn't hope in vain. Similarly, when we as believers practice godliness we can pass the exams that challenge our faith and develop our character. We can walk in confident expectation that God is completing the work He began in us the moment He saved us. (See Phil 1:6.) Our hope is not a disappointment because it is insured by God's love that has been "poured out in our hearts through the Holy Spirit" (v. 5). God's love never lets us down. It will never give out or run dry. "Poured out" embraces the idea of a permanent flood. The Holy Spirit's ministry is to encourage us with the overflowing benefits of God's everlasting love.

We Can Be Reconciled to God
(Rom. 5:6-11)

Reconciliation is another gift God offers us. To be reconciled to God means the hostility between us and God has been resolved and the love relationship has been restored. Notice the way Paul described our reconciliation. He cited our helplessness and wickedness in contrast to Christ's sacrifice. The statement "Christ died for the ungodly" (v. 6) is the central conviction of Christianity. At the cross God's love secured our reconciliation. After I had given an interview to a local TV station regarding the impact of the movie *The Passion of the Christ,* a political official told me that I should speak far less about the cross and much more about the goodwill and peace of Jesus. I replied that if I or anyone else should speak of Jesus apart from the cross, then we remove the atoning sacrifice that makes peace and goodwill a possibility.

What Jesus did on the cross was not merely a demonstration of good will or simply an example of compassion. Paul explained that it is a most unusual thing for someone to give his life for another person. Once in a while someone might die for a good friend. But Jesus gave His life at the cross while we were at war with Him. His sacrifice took place "while we were still sinners" (v. 8). While our transgression was being thrown in His face, Jesus threw our sin on His back. While we owed a debt we couldn't pay, He paid a debt He didn't owe. How can we doubt the love of God when He went to such an extreme to reconcile us to Himself? Significantly, the word "proves" (v. 8) occurs as a present tense verb representing continual action in the Greek. Although the event of the cross happened in the past at an appointed moment, the love of God through the cross continually proves God's disposition toward us today.

The assurance of this truth is explained in Paul's "much more" analogies (vv. 9-10). First, he argued that if Christ has accomplished the work of justifying sinners and reconciling God's enemies, He will surely deliver believers from God's wrath. If the hard work of making sinners into saints has been done, then by comparison how much more we should be assured of His ability to save us from God's wrath. The focus is future. At the end of history when God's holy displeasure will be loosed, believers will be safe from His condemnation. A second "much more" analogy contrasts our pre-conversion status of hostility with our conversion status of reconciliation. The phrase "saved by His life" (v. 10) points to the power of Christ's resurrection and the assurance of our resurrection. If He reconciled us to Himself while we were enemies, how much more will He keep us eternally as His friends? Does this truth make you want to shout for joy? Actually, Paul did break out in jubilation! He used the word "rejoice" (v. 11) as a synonym for jubilant boasting. The idea is one of triumphant exultation and praise. God through Christ has done His part to establish reconciliation. Our part involves the reception of His finished work.

We Can Receive Righteousness
(Rom. 5:12-17)

The repetition of the theme of righteousness is necessary for understanding the big picture of sin. Paul didn't present a detailed analysis of the origin of evil. He simply stated that "sin entered the world through one man" (v. 12). Adam's disobedience opened the door. Although Eve participated also, Adam was the responsible agent. By his free choice Adam sinned against God and brought evil and death into the human race. Notice the phrase "all sinned." Volumes of studies have focused on its meaning. The one sin of the one man was literally the sin of each of us. All of us personally sinned when Adam disobeyed and we are inseparably united to his sin.

Paul pointed out that Adam's sin brought all humanity into the snare of evil and death. But what about those who sinned before the law was given? How can someone be a lawbreaker if there is no law to break? Paul explained that "sin was in the world before the law" (v. 13). The absence of the Mosaic law didn't mean there was no sin. Technically, their sin was not charged to their account because there was no law to define it. (See 3:20.) However, sin is not just a violation of law, it is a rebellion against God. Adam's transgression did violate the command given him by God. Those who lived between the time of Adam and Moses died also, proving that sin was in the world before the Mosaic law and must be more than direct transgressions of the Mosaic law. Adam's rebellion polluted God's creation. Universal sin and death resulted, making the one man, Adam, the father of sin and death.

When Paul wrote that Adam was "a prototype of the Coming One" (v. 14), he was indicating that just as Adam was the head of sinful humanity, Christ is the head of redeemed humanity. The difference between the two, however, is far grater than the similarity.

Remember how Paul used the "much more" analogy earlier? He applied it in verse 15 to reveal the contrast between God's grace and Adam's trespass. A "trespass" implies a deviation or a transgression. Although Adam's deviation affected the whole human race and alienated all of us from God, the gift of God's grace in Christ reversed the curse of death and separation. By the "one man, Jesus Christ," God's grace was much more liberating that Adam's sin was captivating. The result of Adam's trespass leads to a death sentence. The result of God's overflowing grace leads to a life sentence. It is a mistake to think that Paul was teaching universal salvation. Clearly, in this epistle and in his other epistles, Paul went to great length emphasizing that while salvation is a free gift it is a gift that must be received so that a person may experience God's righteousness. Paul engaged the "much more" analogy once again in verse 17 to show that by Adam's sin "death reigned," but by Jesus' redeeming grace, life reigns.

For Your Consideration

1. How much more do you esteem the grandeur of God's grace in comparison to the darkness of your sin?

_____

_____

2. Do you understand that there is more grace in God's heart than there is sin in your life?

_____

_____

We Can Have Eternal Life
(Rom. 5:18-21)

God provides eternal life for us through the "one righteous act" of Christ's atoning sacrifice (v.18). Notice how Paul used a contrast again. Through the one act of disobedience by Adam, the sentence of condemnation covered everyone. Through the one saving act of

Christ, the sentence of "life-giving justification" became available to everyone. Paul was not advocating that Christ's atoning work provides eternal life automatically even if faith in Christ is absent. Paul was clearly not a universalist. His contention was that although everyone is given the opportunity for life eternal with Christ, not everyone will accept it. The provision for "life-giving justification" was settled once and for all at the cross. Our participation in the provision is settled only when by faith we trust Christ for eternal life.

The phrase "many will be made righteous" (v. 19) expresses both a present possibility and a future reality. By using a future tense, Paul was not suggesting that our justification is limited to a future judgment day. He was stating the inevitable consequence of a right relationship that applies to anyone at anytime. Because of Christ's obedience at the cross, Adam's disobedience was overcome and the way was opened so that "many" might be saved. But wait a minute. If righteousness is credited to us by faith, then what role does the moral law play in God's plan of redemption? What was the purpose of the law? Didn't the law of Moses stand between the sin of Adam and the cross of Christ? Paul explained that the law served as a mirror to reveal the magnitude of our sin problem. God gave the law through Moses to make it absolutely plain that all of us are sinners who violate His commands. The law doesn't force us to sin, but it shows that we are in fact sinners. Suppose I find a lake in the woods and decide to fish in it. A sign is posted in clear view that says "No fishing! Violators will be prosecuted!" I ignore the sign and fish anyway only to be arrested an hour later. Should I blame my arrest on the sign? The law, like a sign, is not the problem. The law simply reveals my rebellion against authority.

Paul claimed that although the law exposed the multiplication of sin, God unleashed the exponential advance of grace. When Paul wrote that grace "multiplied even more" (v. 20), he used a single Greek word that means "excessive beyond measure." God's grace trumps human sin every time and it does so in a way that is incomparably greater than we can fathom. The "reign of death" (v. 21) ceases in the presence of the untamed God who introduces the rule of grace. Grace reigns when God credits righteousness to our account through faith in His Son, our Savior. The aim of grace is the experience of abundant and eternal life because of "Jesus Christ our Lord."

God Delivers from Sin

Deliverance (Rom. 6:1-11)

Every distortion of the truth about God carries a detrimental consequence. One Saturday morning I listened to a young lady who distorted Jesus' mandate to "love your enemies" (Matt. 5:44). She was entrenched in spiritual darkness and held captive by the chains of sin. With wild-eyed intensity she exclaimed, "Jesus said, 'love your enemies.' Satan is the enemy of Jesus. So, I love Satan." The tragic fruit of her absurd logic pointed to a life of moral deception and self-destruction.

Paul anticipated that some individuals might distort the doctrine of grace and use it as a license to indulge in sinful practices. He realized the detrimental consequence of misinterpreting and misusing God's gracious act of justification. In response to the claim that "where sin multiplied, grace multiplied even more" (Rom 5:20), Paul discerned that some individuals might conclude that the more you sin, the more

BIBLE TRUTH:
We know God is active in today's world because He delivers believers from sin.

LIFE IMPACT:
To help you depend on God to deliver you from sin

41

grace you get. Consequently, the question "Should we continue in sin in order that grace may multiply?" (v. 1) is answered by an emphatic "Absolutely not!" (v. 2). God's grace does not make sin less serious and His forgiveness does not make sin more inviting. Anyone who excuses and exalts sin at the expense of God's grace portrays a profound distortion of the truth and fails to embrace the deliverance that Jesus provides. Salvation involves both a transaction and a transformation. As a transaction, the atoning death of Christ paid the penalty for our sin and we were made right with God by faith in His Son. As a transformation, the grace of God in Christ empowers us to live righteously so that we might resist sin. Paul utilized the metaphor of death to illustrate this truth. The metaphor should not be pressed beyond its context, however. He was not suggesting that a believer is dead to the attraction of sin. After all, Paul argued convincingly in chapter seven that the struggle against sin is a lifetime battle. The metaphor of death speaks of separation. When an individual becomes a follower of Christ, a separation occurs. The union with sin has been broken and a union with Christ has formed. Death to sin separates a believer from sin's dominion and into Christ's deliverance.

To enhance the emphasis of separation, Paul appealed to the ordinance of baptism. Paul explained that a believer is "buried with Him [Christ] by

A CLOSER LOOK

Baptized

The word "baptized" in 6:3 is more a transliteration than a translation. The word is a form of the Greek *baptizo* and is brought over into English. An accurate translation of the word is "immerse" or "to submerge and emerge." In the first century, baptism was the word chosen to signify the dyeing of a garment or the drawing of water by dipping a vessel into another. Christian baptism is a public act of obedience to Christ and one's profession of faith in Him. The going under and coming up from water symbolizes dying with Christ and rising with Christ.

Biblical Illustrator

Ancient Byzantine baptistry, showing the importance given baptism by the early church (6:3-4).

baptism into death" (v. 4). Baptism is the believer's act of obedience that portrays the separation event. Believers during the first century made a public profession of faith in Christ by being baptized. Baptism presents the external picture of an inner relationship with Christ. The picture of baptism in this passage and throughout the New Testament is consistently one of immersion and identification. Across the centuries, the mode and meaning of baptism have been obscured by inaccurate teaching and practice. Some traditions prefer the mode of sprinkling, but sprinkling is entirely incapable of symbolizing baptism as death and resurrection. Only immersion signifies the total identification of a believer in union with Christ. Although liturgical aspects of baptism are usually associated with tranquility, the word *baptism* in the first century evoked images of violence and death. It was used with reference to ships that sank under water and people who drowned. Jesus used the word *baptism* to refer to His death. (See Mark 10:38.) Clearly, baptism is not a symbol of domestication, but a symbol of termination.

Some traditions contend that the act of baptism is necessary for salvation. Despite the popularity of baptismal regeneration, it is foreign to the New Testament message of salvation by grace. Baptism is a testimony of obedience that affirms salvation, but it is not a meritorious work that achieves salvation.

The death and resurrection of Christ accomplished our redemption. Apart from His saving grace, baptism is a hollow practice. But notice how Paul emphasized the new life that baptism symbolizes. Not only is a believer identified with Christ in the likeness of His death, but also united with Christ in "His resurrection" (v. 5). New life through Christ follows the defeat of sin's reign. The invasion of Christ in a believer's life ends the dominion of sin. The grip of evil is broken and the "old self" expires (v. 6). The term "old self" refers to the old nature under the command of sin.

Paul explained that our old self was nailed to the cross with Christ so that we wouldn't be enslaved to sin any longer. When a slave was crucified, all claims of his master became null and void. A dead slave was freed from his cruel master's dominion. Obviously, he was no longer obligated to carry out the habits of wickedness. Similarly, believers are crucified with Christ and are not obligated to grovel when sin growls. The verb "abolished" (v. 6) in the Greek does not mean that sin has been totally eradicated, but that sin has been disabled. Because of a believer's union with Christ, sin has been deprived of its prevailing mastery. This doesn't mean that we can't sin. It means we are no longer slaves to sin. We are no longer compelled to obey the orders of our sinful self. Jesus provided deliverance from the power of sin by His death and resurrection. In addition, He provides deliverance from the pull of sin as we "live with Him" (v. 8).

The exhilarating reality of this truth is wrapped up in the expression "death no longer rules over Him" (v. 9). On our behalf Jesus submitted to the rule of death. He gave Himself vicariously at the cross so that we might live victoriously for His purpose. Notice the attending expression: "He died to sin once for all" (v. 10). "Once for all" is a single Greek word that denotes a decisive and unrepeatable event. Christ will not die again. His resurrection broke sin's lock

A CLOSER LOOK

Offer

The Greek word for "offer" in Romans 6:13 contains the idea of placing something at someone's disposal or presenting something to someone. Paul used this word in 12:1 of presenting our bodies as living sacrifices. In 6:13 Paul urged believers to place themselves at God's disposal, and the thrust is both negative (what the Christians were doing) and positive (what they should do). Believers are not to make themselves available to sin, but they are to make themselves available to God. The word also is used in 6:19, where Paul contrasted being slaves to sin (what the Christians were) with being slaves to righteousness (what they should be).

and conquered death's prison forever. We will battle sin day after day, but because of Christ's resurrection triumph we can rely on Him for our victory.

Dante's View in Death Valley, California, offers a striking scene. You can look down 282 feet and see a place called Badwater. This is the lowest spot in the Western Hemisphere. From the same spot you can look up and see Mount Whitney, one of the highest peaks in the world. Perspective matters. At the cross we see the lowest degradation of sin. But from that spot we also see the highest grandeur of Christ's grace. If you see yourself as dead to sin but alive to Christ, then you'll move toward the victory platform.

For Your Consideration

1. In a brief statement, how would you describe your battle with sin and self?

———————————————————————————————————

———————————————————————————————————

2. How is sin's dominion over the body abolished?

———————————————————————————————————

———————————————————————————————————

Demand (Rom. 6:12-14,20-23)

When God justifies us by faith in Christ, the grip of the old self controlled by sin is broken. A new relationship begins. Christ expects us to meet the demand of a new way of life. Sin has been dethroned, but it will always attempt to reassert its authority in our lives.

Paul expressed the imperative of verse 12, "Do not let sin reign in your mortal body," to remind us that we have a choice and a responsibility. Sin has no authority to control a believer unless the believer chooses to "obey its desires." Truly we have died to sin, but sin has not died to us. As believers we are alive to Christ, but we work out the details of godliness while still in the flesh. The desires and urges of the body are receptacles for sin. Any part of the body can become a warhead for sin. Paul was not arguing that the body is the *cause* of sin, but that it is a *conduit* for sin.

The idea is that sin wages war in the theater of our flesh, and the believer must be on guard not to allow the desires of the flesh to become a weapon for the enemy. Instead, we are commended to offer all the parts of our body "to God as weapons for righteousness" (v. 13). A believer fully surrendered to God strikes fear in Satan's army. When we yield all that we are to all of God's purpose we become missiles for His holiness.

Believers are not slaves to sin. We present our bodies to God for righteousness because His grace liberated us from sin's clutch and from the law's condemnation. The law can rebuke and revile, but it cannot redeem. God's saving grace is a sanctifying grace that empowers believers to respond triumphantly over sin's treachery. Paul applied the slave analogy once more to clarify and emphasize the truth. We are now to engage in living for Christ as passionately as we were passionate about living for sin before. Having turned away from slavery to unrighteousness, believers willingly embrace slavery to godliness.

The fruit of sin is worthless and it points toward death. The fruit of sanctification is priceless and points toward eternal life. Here's the bottom line. Sin pays wages that result in death. God gives His Son who offers life forever. "Wages" denote a payment earned. "Gift" denotes a present freely extended. The gift of "eternal life in Christ Jesus our Lord" (v. 23) is offered to everyone, regardless of status. But the gift only becomes personally applicable when it's received by faith.

Grace is free, but it is not cheap! Jesus Christ paid the cost of salvation to enable believers to pay the cost of discipleship.

For Your Consideration

1. In what specific ways do you find that sin still tries to dictate your behavior?

2. Think about your life before Christ saved you. Think about the things you pursued and the behavior you practiced. When you compare the old life with the new life, how do you process the shame that sometimes revisits you?

Difficulty (Rom. 7:12-23)

Have you ever walked past a sign that said WET PAINT, DO NOT TOUCH? Didn't you just want to check and see if it was dry? The command not to touch conflicted with a desire inside of you. The difficulty we encounter is a spiritual war-between-the-states. The state of our new life in Christ will always be in conflict with our human nature and the appeal of sin. So where does the difficulty begin? Is the law the real problem?

Paul argued that the difficulty begins with sin and the real problem is not the law. Sin is deceptive. It will even use the law as a tool to achieve destruction. The law is not the cause of spiritual death but the law reveals and arouses sin. The law defines and describes sin. Paul explained that "the law is holy, and the commandment is holy" (v. 12). The reason the law is holy is God gave it and He is holy. Sin, however, used the law as a tool to bring out death and in doing so sin exposed its own identity as corrupt "beyond measure (v. 13).

With refreshing candor Paul discussed the struggle between his desire to live righteously for Christ and his failure to overcome sin's power. His struggle is also a representative experience for every believer. Sanctification is a life-long process of spiritual growth that moves a believer away from dependency on self and toward a dependency on the Spirit. Along the way, however, are victories and defeats.

Paul confessed that he didn't always understand his own behavior. He humbly admitted, "I do not practice what I want to do" (v. 15). Instead, he found

LEARNING ACTIVITY

Wet Paint, Do Not Touch

Read the commentary for Romans 7:12-23. What are some things you are most tempted to say, do, or think even though you know they are wrong? List some of those things God brings to your mind below.

himself practicing the very thing he hated. Was the law responsible for the failure? Not at all. The law was good because it reminded Paul about God's perfect standard and Paul's inability to live up to it. The problem involved the infiltration of sin into every motive, decision, and action of his life. The desire to live righteously was present, but the "ability to do it" (v. 18) was insufficient. Paul was not saying that a believer is totally incapable of doing anything good. He was explaining that a believer is unable to completely fulfill the requirements of God's law. When Paul looked at God's standard he saw holy perfection. When he looked at himself he saw sinful imperfection. Paul's transparent confession speaks deeply to my own heart. The more I grow in conformity to Christ, the more I am compelled to realize my need to grow.

LEARNING ACTIVITY

Deliverance

Does your life reflect your believing you are delivered from sin? Complete the following sentence with those things you think should be different in your life because God has delivered you from the bondage of sin.

If I am delivered from sin, then ...

_____

_____

Scan the psalms to find chapters or verses that reflect your being delivered. Personalize some of the verses to pray and praise God for His deliverance.

_____

_____

_____

The deeper I go in a love relationship with Jesus, the more I am frustrated by my disobedience. The further I journey in discipleship, the clearer I see the sin that poisons my heart.

The ongoing presence of evil in believers' lives led Paul to conclude that a universal principle was at work. Two forces wage war in the soul. One delights in the law of God. The other despises the law of God. Our sinful nature will always fight against our renewed nature. Was Paul dodging personal responsibility for sin by saying "I am no longer the one doing it" (vv. 17,20)? To the contrary, he had already stated his participation in wrongdoing. Paul accepted responsibility, but he made clear that indwelling sin has the power to control our identity.

Deliverer (Rom. 7:24-25)

We are helpless if we battle sin alone. We are hopeless if we battle sin with the law. We need a deliverer. When Paul cried "What a wretched man I am!" (v. 24), he expressed the futility of trying to achieve victory over sin by living good enough. Can you identify with Paul's painful admission? The fatal flaw of sin has doomed us. I grieved to watch the space shuttle *Columbia* splinter across a February sky. Lives were lost and the nation was shocked. Later, NASA engineers determined that a 2 ½ pound piece of insulation striking the left wing of the shuttle was the fatal flaw. Nothing could be done by anyone once the *Columbia* tried to come home. In a similar way we have been struck by a fatal flaw. There is nothing humanly possible that can be done to change the outcome. We are wretched apart from our Holy Deliverer. Victory over sin's power and Satan's plan comes only through Jesus Christ. Consequently, Paul shouted his gratitude to "Jesus Christ our Lord!" (v. 25).

Paul conceded that he was a slave to two laws. His mind loved the law of God but his flesh loved the law of sin. When you sit down on an airplane in preparation for a flight, the law of gravity applies. Once the engines roar and the plane reaches a certain speed another law takes over—the law of aerodynamics. The plane lifts high above the ground and soars into the sky. Similarly, both the law of sin and the law of grace operate on believers. When we are in a plane above the clouds the law of gravity does not cease to exist, and when we walk through life the law of sin does not cease. The important thing to remember is that the law of God's grace can overpower the law of sin like the law of aerodynamics overpowers the law of gravity. Hallelujah for our Deliverer!

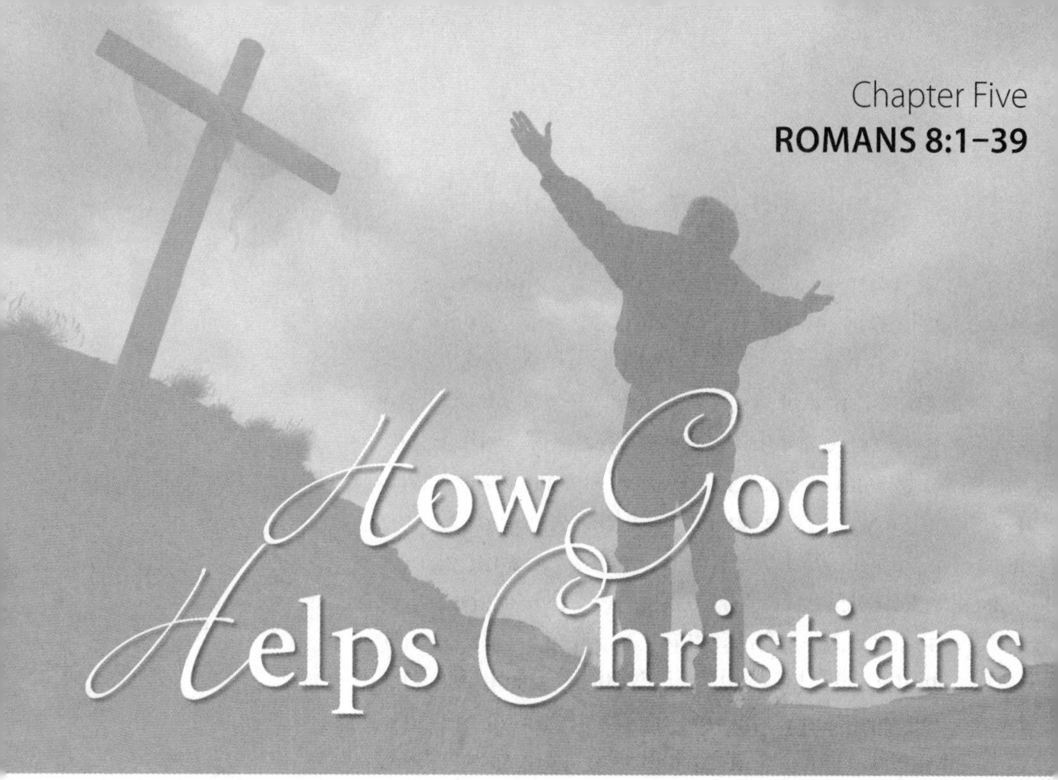

Chapter Five

ROMANS 8:1–39

How God Helps Christians

BIBLE TRUTH:
God gives evidence He cares about us by all He does on behalf of Christians.

LIFE IMPACT:
To help you show your awareness of God's care for you

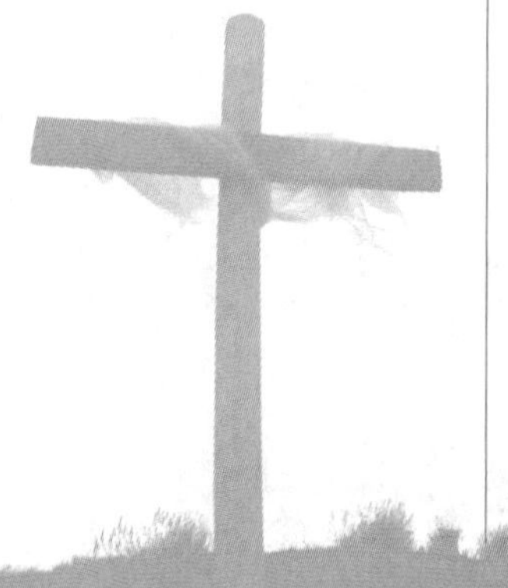

God Sets Us Free from Death (Rom. 8:1-11)

Many of us harbor an awkward guilt that torments our conscience. At unexpected moments it pierces us with accusation. Privately, we hear an incriminating voice that whispers "what if?" What if God is really ticked because of my habit? What if somewhere in my past I turned my back on God? What if I stepped over the line and spurned God's mercy? The "what if" list goes on.

Paul described the struggle between our old and new natures in the latter half of Romans 7, and he drew a staggering conclusion. God accepts us by faith and delivers us from sin's captivity. We don't have to guess how He feels about us. We don't have to wonder about any "what if" lurking in the shadows. God cares so much that He wants us to realize that "no condemnation now exists for those in Christ Jesus"

LEARNING ACTIVITY

Who Cares?

What can make you feel someone does not care about you?

_____

_____

How do you know when someone does care for you?

_____

_____

How do you know God cares for you?

_____

_____

(v. 1). The reason for "no condemnation" is our union "in Christ." God exonerates believers at the moment of conversion. The decree of eternal death is removed. But what about the consequences of our sin? How do we distinguish between consequences and condemnation? Consequences are the results of our sinful choices. They are the effects that logically follow wrong actions. Believers do indeed suffer the consequences of their sin. Condemnation, however, refers to the verdict of eternal doom pronounced upon humanity by God. Because believers have been justified by faith in Christ, they do not suffer condemnation.

Furthermore, believers have a powerful new law operating within them called the "law of life in Christ Jesus" (v. 2). As the Holy Spirit indwells our lives, He enables us to walk in victory rather than in defeat. Obviously, the law cannot insure triumph over death or victory over sin. The law cannot provide deliverance because it is "limited by the flesh" (v. 3). The problem is not the law; the problem is the weakness of the flesh. Think about it like this: A yardstick can measure how tall you are, but it can't make you grow. Similarly, the law can offer you a moral measurement, but it can't make you righteous before God. The law could not save then and it cannot save now. Consequently, God acted redemptively "by sending His own Son in flesh like ours" (v. 3).

Notice in verse 3 the emphasis on the word "own." God didn't send an angel and He didn't send a mere man. He sent "His own Son" incarnate in human flesh as a "sin offering." The phrase "sin offering" expresses the amazing substitutionary aspect of the atonement. Jesus was sinless; we are sinful. He assumed our humanity but never once succumbed to sin. On the cross Jesus took our sin and by His death accomplished what the law could never do. The law of God required perfection and justice. Jesus satisfied the demand of perfection by His sinless life, and He satisfied the necessity of justice by dying for our sins.

Consequently, when we place our faith in Christ, "the law's requirement" (v. 4) is accomplished in us by the work of the Holy Spirit. Before we trust Christ we live in constant defeat by sin. When He saves us, however, the Holy Spirit becomes resident in us to enable us to live triumphantly "according to the Spirit."

Paul portrayed the differences between a believer in Christ and an unbeliever by means of three contrasts. First, there is a difference of concentration. The absorbing interest of an unbeliever revolves around the "things of the flesh," but a believer longs to focus on the "things of the Spirit" (v. 5).

Second, there is a difference of consummation. A person devoted to the things of the flesh, things contrary to or removed from God, can reap only one reward: "death." In contrast, a person devoted to the things of the Spirit reaps a reward of "life and peace" (v. 6).

Third, there is a difference of cooperation. The disposition of an unbeliever is hostile to God and unwilling to submit to God's law. (See v. 7.) The response of a believer, however, is a desire to please God because His Spirit dwells within anyone who belongs to Christ. The presence and dominance of the Holy Spirit is impossible without faith in Christ, and faith in Christ is impossible without the convicting and enabling power of the Holy Spirit. Consequently, Paul explained "if anyone does not have the Spirit of Christ, he does not belong to him" (v. 9).

The Holy Spirit resides in believers and thus we have the confidence that we can live victoriously without condemnation because Christ has set us free from eternal death. Although our "mortal bodies" (v. 11) will suffer death, our Heavenly Father will raise us to life just as He raised His Son, our Savior, from the tomb.

God's Spirit Leads Us
(Rom. 8:12-17)

The Holy Spirit is mentioned 19 times in Romans 8. Paul emphasized the absolute necessity of the Spirit's leadership in our lives. Paul prompts believers to realize that we no longer have an obligation to the flesh. The word "obligated" (v. 12) refers to a debt owed. Believers do not owe any spiritual capital to the bank of the flesh. We are under no orders to indulge in sinful appetites and satisfy immoral desires. Clearly, we will face temptations our entire lives and may occasionally succumb to sins of the flesh, but the habitual pattern will be a life influenced by the Holy Spirit. Our inability to conquer sin by ourselves is illustrated by our need to depend on the Spirit to "put to death the deeds of the body" (v. 13). Obeying the leadership of the Holy Spirit is the distinguishing mark of a believer. The Spirit indwells, empowers, and enables believers to put away the deeds of the body. Consequently Paul exclaimed, "All those led by God's Spirit are God's sons" (v. 14). In contrast are unbelievers who are still controlled by their sinful nature and remain outside God's family.

Paul referred to the Graeco-Roman practice of adoption to underscore our new relationship in the family of God. When adoption occurred, all old debts were cancelled and the adoptee was granted full rights and privileges in a family to which he did not belong by nature. All previous relationships were severed and a new affection emerged whereby the individual could approach the head of the family as father. Paul explained that, as believers, we can approach our heavenly Father as *"Abba"* (v. 15). The Aramaic word *Abba* is a tender expression similar to our word "daddy" or "papa." The term reflects the intimacy stirred in our hearts by the Holy Spirit. Witnesses were always present during an official Roman adoption ceremony. The Holy Spirit serves as a witness to authenticate our status in a new family. Consequently, He "testifies together with our spirit that we are God's children" (v. 16). Furthermore, when an adoption occurred the adoptee was entitled to the same inheritance as any other child in the family. Applying this metaphor to believers, Paul emphasized that we are not only "heirs," but "co-heirs with Christ" (v. 17). Everything that belongs to Jesus belongs to us as adopted children. This includes the sufferings and trials of living for Him in the present world as well as the delight of His glory in the next.

For Your Consideration
1. What thoughts surge through your mind when you contemplate being a child in God's family?

---

2. In what ways are you being led by God's Spirit
   in your daily decisions?

_____

_____

_____

_____

God's Spirit Strengthens Us
(Rom. 8:18-27)

Because God's Spirit strengthens us we can endure
any present suffering with eager expectation about
the future. Our heavenly destiny does not negate our
earthly trials. Paul considered that "the sufferings of
this present time are not worth comparing with the
glory that is going to be revealed to us" (v. 18). The
word "considered" is not a supposition, but a fixed
conclusion based on reasonable calculation.

God's Spirit strengthens us to endure our present problems with a fixed focus on a future glory.
Included in this glory is the redemption of creation.
The whole earth has suffered because of human sin
and has been "subjected to futility" (v. 20). Genesis
3:17-19 testifies to the effects of sin on the physical
world. When God placed the earth under the dominion of man, God subjected it to the consequences of
human choices. Despite the abuse and corruption
of creation through human sin, the earth will share
the benefits of a redemption similar to that which
believers experience.

Paul compared the transformation of the created order to the anticipation of childbirth. He explained that the entire creation has been in travail "with labor pains until now" (v. 22), but God is preparing a new birth for His creation. He has something far better in the future than we now experience in the present. Because we have "the Spirit as the firstfruits" (v. 23), we are guaranteed that His promise will not fail. The term "firstfruits" refers to bringing the first of the harvests and consecrating it to God. (See Lev. 23:10-11.) "Firstfruits" indicates there will be more fruit and a better harvest. It represents a foretaste of a greater dimension.

A CLOSER LOOK

"More than Victorious"

Our English word "victorious" comes from the Greek verb *nikao* and the Greek noun *nike*. The phrase "more than victorious" ("conquerors," KJV) in verse 37 is actually a single word that combines the prefix hyper with the first person plural verb *nikomen* and the result is *hypernikomen*. By using the intense form of the word "victorious," Paul emphasized the triumphant life believers can experience because of Christ's love. We don't merely survive. We thrive because of the extravagant love Christ provides.

Can you apply the metaphor? The Holy Spirit strengthening our lives represents a foretaste of what God has in store for believers. The groaning we experience is an inner longing for the ultimate phase of our adoption—the redemption of our bodies. That's why we occasionally feel we don't belong here. That's why we have a periodic homesickness for a place called heaven even though we've never been there. Our salvation includes a hope that our bodies will one day experience a complete transformation. Since we hope for something unseen, we need patience as we wait. The Spirit strengthens us to endure.

Another way the Spirit helps us is in regard to prayer. Do you occasionally feel inadequate when you pray? How many times have you struggled to discern how to pray for someone? "Weakness" in verse 26 is not synonymous with sin and suffering. It refers to our human limitations. We don't see things clearly. We are limited in our understanding of motives and objectives when we pray. We are weak and in need of the Holy Spirit to intercede for us. He knows us intimately. He also knows "the will of God" perfectly (v. 27). The Spirit never contradicts the will of God or the Word of God. He intercedes in ways that are too deep for language to fathom, but always for God's glory in our lives.

For Your Consideration

Consider all your heartaches, troubles, and agonies. Write them down on one side of a ledger. Then consider all that you have to look forward to in heaven where faith becomes sight and anticipation meets realization. Write those truths on the opposite side of the ledger. What conclusions do you draw?

God Sides with Us (Rom. 8:28-39)

I have often been driven to my knees bewildered by a burden I couldn't comprehend only to discover that God was designing a blessing I couldn't deny. Many of us have relied on the truth that "all things work together for the good of those who love God" (v. 28). This memorable verse does not claim that "all things just happen to work out." "Things" don't work at all. Things are incapable of autonomous action. A variant reading in the Greek text says "God works together in all things." God is the subject in all translations. God is the Sovereign One who sides with us to transform burdens into blessings and difficulties into doors. The extended phrase "those who love God; those who are called according to His purpose" explains that the application centers on believers. The "good" that God designs for believers refers to vital and ultimate good. Our perspective regarding "good" is not necessarily the same as God's idea of good. Consequently, we must always add to our perspective the statement "according to His purpose." God's purpose for believers is beautifully illustrated by the verbs "foreknew," "predestined," "conformed," justified," and glorified" (vv. 29-30).

The doctrine of predestination can be puzzling. Some commentators believe it means the elect are those God has chosen for salvation. Others con-

LEARNING ACTIVITY

Care Package

Describe a situation in your life today in which you have become aware of God's care for you.

_____

_____

If you had to compile a "care package" to symbolize God's care, what items would you place in it? List the items below.

_____

_____

Choose one of the items to place in a visible place as a reminder of God's care for you. Use the item as a talking point to share your awareness of God's care for you with others.

_____

_____

tend that predestination also refers to those God has chosen for damnation. I have found it wise to avoid arguing for more than the Bible teaches about the doctrine and to avoid minimizing all that the Bible clearly affirms about it. God's truth is designed to challenge us, but not to confuse us. In the context of Romans

8:28-29 the word "predestine" is not related to salvation, but to sanctification. The concern is not conversion, but conformity. God in His sovereignty predestined us to be "conformed to the image of His Son" (v. 29). Think about it like this: The Greek origin for "predestined" comes from the practice of marking a boundary before the horizon. Similarly, God established a boundary regarding His purpose. Not everyone will enter heaven. Only those who trust His Son are within the boundary of His saving grace. Consequently, long before the sun ever beamed its rays on the first horizon, God determined that those who receive His salvation should live in moral conformity to His Son. We, who by faith have been adopted into God's family, are challenged to live as siblings ("brothers") resembling the "firstborn" who is our Lord Jesus Christ. God's activity of foreknowledge, predestination, calling, and justification climaxes with glorification. Are you wondering why "glorified" (v. 30) is translated in the past tense? The reason for the past tense is that God's purpose in siding with believers can be viewed as certain and complete. What God begins, He finishes! God's splendor shines in those whom He saves, and one day His children will experience the ultimate glorification.

Therefore, Paul concluded that because God sides with us no person or circumstance can succeed in siding against us. God declares us righteous and there is no higher authority to claim otherwise. Jesus died on our behalf to set us free from condemnation and no one can vanquish His victory.

Believers will face "affliction, anguish, persecution, famine, nakedness, danger, and sword" but not without the "love of Christ" (v. 35). Whatever God brings us to, He will bring us through! The phrase "we are more than victorious" (v. 37) comes from a single Greek word expressing super conquest. Because of Christ's love we can face hardships and heartbreaks like champions. No supernatural force, no uncertainty of life, no prospect of death, and no dimension of the universe has "the power to separate us from the love of God that is in Christ Jesus our Lord" (v. 39). This chapter opened with the sterling affirmation of "no condemnation" and it concludes with the golden ascertain of "no separation" for a believer.

God's Attitude Toward Israel

Consider God's Mercy
(Rom. 9:1-6,14-24)

Paul concluded the previous chapter by rejoicing in the assurance of God's care and provision for believers. In Romans 9 he probed the heartbreaking problem of those who decline to place their faith in Christ. Of particular concern to Paul was the situation of his own kinsmen, the people of Israel.

To express his intense emotional conviction, Paul made two bold assertions. First, he explained that his conviction was rooted in an accountable relationship to Christ and that his conscience was informed by the Holy Spirit. Second, he asserted that he was willing (if it were possible) to be cursed and separated from Christ if it would mean the salvation of Israel.

BIBLE TRUTH:
God gives evidence He cares about us by His attitude toward Israel.

LIFE IMPACT:
To help you express your assurance of God's care for you

For Your Consideration
Can you identify with Paul's burden regarding the salvation of his fellow citizens? In what ways have you agonized and prayed about family members who have rejected Christ?

_____

_____

_____

_____

_____

Paul's readiness to endure hell on behalf of his unbelieving countrymen is a strong portrayal of his burden. Paul then appealed to the spiritual heritage of Israel as evidence for God's care. He listed several historic blessings to emphasize God's mercy. The Israelites were adopted by God as a special people chosen to carry out His purpose. God's favor on them was manifested by His glory in a way not granted to other nations. Furthermore, God initiated several "covenants" (v. 4) with Israel. At strategic moments in their history, His faithfulness was recorded by covenants with Noah (Gen. 9:9), Abraham (Gen. 17:2), Moses (Ex. 24:8) and David (2 Sam. 23:5). He also gave to them the law as a privilege for their possession and practice. In addition, God entrusted to them the regulations for worship in the temple, as well as hundreds of promises of His deliverance and blessings. The Israelites could also rejoice in their "forefathers" (v. 5), whose leadership and example pointed others to God. Best of all, the Messiah came through the "physical descent" of the Jewish people. The statement "God over all, blessed forever. Amen!" is a clear testimony to the deity of Jesus incarnate through the lineage of Israel.

Paul anticipated a criticism his countrymen would level: God has chosen the people of Israel as His special people and to be the people through whom He would send the Messiah. Yet most of them rejected the Messiah and the salvation He offered. Had God's word failed? Had God's intention for the people of Israel been frustrated forever? In response Paul explained, "it is not as though the Word of God has failed" (v. 6). God always keeps His promise. His promise was not made on the basis of physical bloodline, but on the basis of His sovereign mercy. Spiritual kinship by faith rather than ethnic origin by birth determined who was a true Israelite and a child of Abraham.

Another criticism Paul anticipated was the charge that God does not act fairly in His choices. The question, "Is there injustice with God?" (v. 14), receives a vehement retort of "Absolutely not." It is not possible for God, who is perfect in all His attributes, to behave unjustly. He would violate His own character if He exercised injustice in dealing with anyone. Instead, God shows mercy and compassion. God does not unjustly condemn unbelievers, but in mercy He does save believers. God's freedom to practice mercy is not limited to any class or race of people. He is free and sovereign and His mercy "does not depend on human will or effort" (v. 16).

Pharaoh, who ruled one of the most powerful dynasties in history, deserved death. But God allowed Pharaoh to reign so that He could demonstrate His holy sovereignty over Pharaoh's status. (See v. 17.) Indeed, God hardened Pharaoh's heart, but Pharaoh also hardened his own heart. God gave him opportunities to repent, but Pharaoh refused and thereby hardened himself against God's authority. (See Ex. 7:13,22; 8:15.) God was not unjust toward Pharaoh. Throughout Scripture, God's hardening of an individual is always linked to the consequence of sin. Before God ever hardens someone, that person has declined offers of mercy. The mercy and grace of God

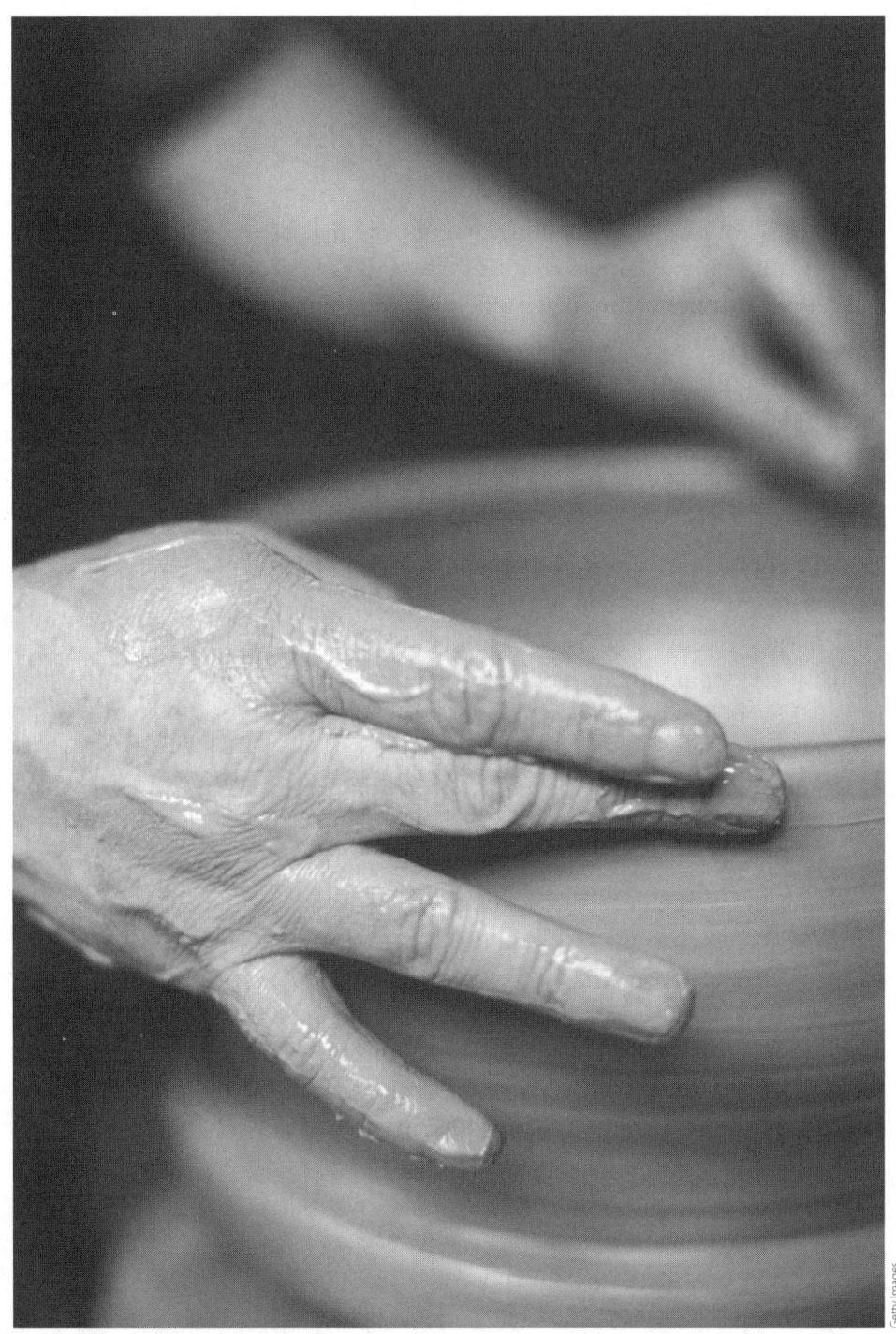

Getty Images

is the foundation for the biblical doctrine of election. We all are equally undeserving of God's favor. We all are equally deserving of God's condemnation. God is not answerable to us for what He does or for whom He uses in His divine plan.

The natural tendency of our logic is to argue that we are not culpable and responsible for our sinful behavior. How would you answer a friend who said, "If God is going to carry out His purpose anyway, then why should He blame me for my sin?" Regrettably, we challenge God with the question, "Why did you make me like this?" Paul anticipated this criticism also, but responded with an illustration regarding the potter and the clay. (See v. 21.) As finite created beings, we cannot call the Creator to give an account for His infinite knowledge and authority. Just as the potter has authority to create from the clay any design he wishes, so also God has the ultimate authority to shape individuals according to His pleasure. Truly, God is sovereign, but He does not abuse His sovereignty. It is not unfair for God to shape individuals for different functions. Their function follows His sovereign design which we are incapable of understanding completely. Paul contended that what we can affirm is that God's patience and mercy shine against the backdrop of His wrath against sin. God acts "to make known the riches of His glory on objects of mercy" (v. 23). God displays His patience so that unbelievers might see His splendor being poured out on believers who by faith are vessels of His mercy. Both Gentiles and Jews are recipients of His favor.

Consequently, Paul drew two conclusions regarding God's purpose and Israel. First, God's redeeming purpose is not confined to the Jews, but embraces the Gentiles who never had the Old Testament law to guide them. Second, despite the privileges his countrymen enjoyed, only a remnant accepted justification by faith in Christ. Most of Israel then and many Jews today practice a righteousness based on human performance instead of a righteousness based on God's grace. Righteousness through Christ's atoning work served as a stumbling block because it denied them the satisfaction of earning their own salvation.

Consider God's Desire (Rom. 10:1-4,8-18,21)

God's desire for Israel's salvation provides evidence that He cares. Furthermore, His offer of salvation to everyone on the same basis of faith in Christ loudly confirms His loving kindness. Unfortunately, many of the Jews spurned God's offer and chose instead to approach God based on their own merit. Their rejection of Jesus as Messiah deeply wounded Paul. The deep longing of his heart was for them to experience salvation. Paul gave testimony that his fellow Israelites committed three serious errors. First, they were guilty of misguided zeal. The statement "They have zeal for God, but not according to knowledge" (v. 2) indicates a willful disregard of true righteousness. They were enthusiastically active about religion, but they had no clear insight about a saving relationship with Christ.

Second, they refused the "righteousness from God" (v. 3). Paul's countrymen in Israel were not much different than many Americans today who disregard the work of Christ for salvation. Paul made it strikingly clear that the righteousness from God came by way of Christ's atoning sacrifice for sin.

Third, the Jews attempted to "establish their own righteousness" (v. 3). The phrase "their own" expresses both a personal indictment and a possessive origin. The "righteousness" they possessed was one they created by their own effort, not one they received from placing their faith in Christ. Submitting to God's righteousness involves trusting His Son as Savior. By submitting to God's righteousness, a person gives up all efforts at self-righteousness. Paul knew from personal experience that any attempt to establish righteousness by means other than God's saving grace is a mark of religious futility.

What did Paul mean by the statement "Christ is the end of the law" (v. 4)? Didn't he previously explain that the law was good? Some interpreters

A CLOSER LOOK

Preach

The word "preach" (Rom. 10:15) comes from the Greek word *kerusso* and it occurs over 60 times in the New Testament. In classical Greek it denoted the act of proclaiming a message that had been commissioned by a ruler or by a person of superior authority. At no time was the preacher or *kerux* allowed to change the message or freelance the announcement he was given. Today's preachers who faithfully fulfill their New Testament function must always speak the authority of God's Word.

contend that the end of the law refers to the fulfillment of the law in the work of Christ. Others maintain that the end of the law refers to its termination. The work of Christ terminated the era of the law as a means of righteousness. Either view is inseparably linked to the phrase "everyone who believes." Christ is certainly the fulfillment of the law, but He is emphatically the end of the law as a way of attaining a right standing before God. Indeed, the law was good because it revealed human sin in light of God's standard and it functioned to point people to Christ. The saving work of Christ brought to a close all the meticulous and exhausting efforts of trying to attain a right standing by keeping the law. In Christ alone we are made right with God because Christ fulfilled the laws demand and ended its claim.

Consequently, the message of salvation rests on two foundational convictions: (1) "Jesus is Lord" and (2) "God raised Him from the dead" (v. 9). The first conviction exalts the absolute authority of Jesus. His ownership over life, death, time, and eternity is paramount. The second conviction validates His deity. The resurrection of Jesus from the dead is God's authentication to us that Jesus is His son. Believing with our hearts and confessing with our mouths are two parts of the same saving experience, not two separate processes.

Those who genuinely embrace the truth about Jesus are not ashamed to go public with their conviction. Furthermore, God saves without "distinction between Jew and Greek" (v. 12). God does not have different methods of saving grace for different nationalities. Paul explained in Romans 3:23 that there is no distinction of sin between nationalities, and here he affirmed that there is no distinction of salvation between them. The free offer of salvation by grace applies clearly and emphatically to every tribe and nation through the statement, "everyone who calls on the name of the Lord will be saved" (v. 13).

For Your Consideration

If God will save everyone who calls on His name, then why doesn't everyone call on the name of the Lord? What hinders people from accepting His offer?

Paul explained with simple, progressive logic that only those who call on the Lord Jesus can be saved. Only those who believe in Him call on Him. Only those who have heard about His saving work can believe in Him. Only those who have a preacher or messenger can hear the gospel and only the

LEARNING ACTIVITY

Rebellious Children

Scan Psalm 106:6-43 noting examples of Israel's rebellion against God. Underline phrases or write words below describing such.

How do people rebel against God today? Prayerfully think about how you rebel against God today.

How does God's mercy toward Israel give you assurance of His care for you?

preacher or messenger sent by God can fulfill the purpose of the salvation event.

The words "preacher" (v. 14) and "preach" (v. 15) come from a Greek word that means to be a herald or to proclaim a message. Preaching the gospel did not originate in the genius of man, but in the authority and wisdom of God. Anyone who witnesses to an unbeliever and testifies about the gospel also operates as a herald under a holy compulsion. Isaiah prophesied of a day when heralds would run into Jerusalem announcing Israel's deliverance form captivity and bondage. (See Isa. 52:7.) Similarly, Paul contended that as heralds of truth, preachers specifically and believers generally carry the message of liberation from sin's bondage. But many of the Jews, if not most of them, declined Christ's offer of freedom and forgiveness. Liberation from sin's prison does not come by religious ritual or by mystical experience, but by hearing and exercising faith in the "message about Christ" (v. 17).

The Israelites could not argue that they had not heard the message about Christ, however. Their rejection had nothing to do with any lack of opportunity to hear it. Their rejection was based on willful disobedience. The Israelites could not argue that God didn't care. The compassion of God resounds in the plea, "All day long I have spread out My hands to a disobedient and defiant people" (v. 21). God's outstretched arms form the perfect image of redeeming love, especially through His Son who stretched His arms on a splintered cross and cried "I love you" to the whole world.

Consider God's Patience
(Rom. 11:1-2,5-6,11-12,25-26a)

The gravity of Israel's rejection of God's Son could not be denied. The people's persistent refusal to place their faith in Christ signaled a widening gap between their privileges and God's promises. The idea of God discarding Israel, however, received a firm reply of "Absolutely not" (v. 1). God reaffirmed His overriding patience and once again gave evidence of His relentless care and righteous longsuffering.

Paul pointed out that he, too, was an Israelite and God had not excluded him from redeeming love. Paul's own conversion made it obvious that God had not rejected all Israelites. The possibility of God rejecting Israel from His divine plan was inconceivable because God would have to deny His foreknowledge. Because God foreknew and predetermined to set His special blessing on Israel, He can never totally dismiss them.

One of the clearest evidences that God has not rejected Israel is the remnant of Jews whom God has graciously saved and commissioned to serve Him. Paul cited an incident from the life of Elijah (see 1 Kings 19:18) to prove that God always has a remnant of individuals who trust Him and maintain a passion for His glory. Paul emphasized that the present remnant was "chosen by grace" (v. 5). The words "chosen" and "grace" refer to the sovereignty of God's love. His purpose is not vanquished by a majority who deny Him. A remnant is not merely a haphazard combination of individuals who practice

LEARNING ACTIVITY

Blessed Assurance

How do you best express your thoughts and feelings? Is it through written or spoken words, music, art, or nature? Describe how you can use one of your favorite means to express your assurance of God's care for you.

Set aside a specific time and/or place to express this assurance during the coming week.

piety, but a people chosen by God and saved by grace. A remnant does not exist because of its merit or character, but because of God's saving and sustaining power.

The contrast between grace and works is crucial to God's purpose. Do you understand why divine grace and human works are incompatible in the saving event? Grace occupies the exclusive place in salvation. If entitlement and prerogative play a role in salvation then there is no point in speaking about grace. Otherwise "grace ceases to be grace" (v. 6) and God's patience is pointless. Thankfully, God's patience stands like a beacon in the long night of Israel's rebellion. Although the nation had hardened itself in unbelief, the people had not stumbled beyond recovery. How amazed are you at God's continual patience? Can you describe a time when you stumbled and God brought you through it?

The result of Israel's stumble became the occasion for salvation to the Gentiles. God used Israel's rejection as both a platform to reach others and as an incentive to make the nation "jealous" (v. 11) for His gift of grace. Regrettably, we who embrace the gift of God have not lived up to the goal of making the Jews desire what we enjoy. Nevertheless, Israel's loss became the Gentiles' gain and brought "riches for the world" (v. 12). The word "riches" in this context denotes an abundance of blessings for others. Despite Israel's failure, Paul anticipated a time when the nation's faith in Christ would inaugurate a blessing to the world far in excess of anything previously imagined. He envisioned a time when "all Israel will be saved" (v. 26). Obviously, Israel's salvation would be on the same basis as that of other races, namely, faith in Jesus as the Son of God and Messiah. Some commentators understand "all Israel" literally, others understand the phrase to mean "spiritual Israel." Paul looked forward to the day when the entire nation of Israel would find its place in God's redemptive plan, a day when all the people would experience God's patience in restoring them.

Respect God's Will

Discern God's Will
(Rom. 12:1-2)

When I was a young believer, thoughts about the will of God left me more confused than confirmed. I wasn't sure if God's will was a mystery to be solved or a misery to be accepted. After several years of walking in His grace and growing in His word, I realized that God's will was not a secret He was hiding but a plan He was revealing. Unfortunately, some believers want God to display His will before they decide to obey His will. Respecting God's will, however, involves a commitment to embrace it regardless of personal preference or comfort. Suppose I drive into the parking lot of a shopping mall. I stop my car and roll down my window near the door of a retail store. I cup my hands over my mouth and shout earnestly, "Open door! Please open!" Obviously, anyone nearby would think I was acting weird. The door won't open just because I prefer

BIBLE TRUTH:
Believers are to respect God's will, which involves discerning and doing it in all aspects of their lives.

LIFE IMPACT:
To help you live for God by following His will in all aspects of your life

to look inside the store before entering it. I must first make a commitment. So I park my car, get out and walk to the entrance. At the appropriate moment the sensor on the automatic door activates a signal that opens the door for me to enter. The analogy is practical and obvious. Sometimes we sit in the parking lot of life and shout for God to open the door of His will. We would rather observe what's behind the door first. We want to investigate and evaluate before we actually walk inside the store of God's will. However, God never reveals His will at the request of our disobedience. Instead, when we walk toward His purpose and follow where He leads, He discloses His desire and opens the appropriate doors exactly when needed.

Paul urged believers to discern and obey the Lord's will by placing their bodies on God's altar of service and by allowing their minds to be transformed. The word "urge" is a tender command motivated by the "mercies of God" (v. 1). The plural form of mercy may seem unusual, but Paul was emphasizing the numerous blessings and benefits that God freely gives to believers.

By urging the Christians in Rome to offer their entire lives in service to God's will, Paul was expressing the connection between ethics and theology. God cares how we live, and He expects us to honor His will by presenting our bodies for His glory. The word "present" in the Greek relates to the practice of sacrificing an animal. In the Old Testament sacrificial system only a live animal could be dedicated to God. Borrowing from the rich imagery of his ancestry, Paul linked the pursuit of God's will with a deliberate act of sacrifice. As worshipers we are called to yield our bodies as holy instruments upon God's altar so that we may please Him. By living sacrificially for His truth and obeying His commands we reinforce the event of passionate worship and we experience God's pleasure. Have you considered that the will of God is never divorced from the worship of God? Furthermore, have you discovered that the will of God for us is never isolated from the pleasure of God in us?

A second aspect of discerning God's will involves the transformation of our minds. A righteous change in the way we think begins by resisting the way the world thinks. We are challenged as followers of Christ to resist being "conformed to this age" (v. 2). Paul explained elsewhere that "this age" or cultural system stands in contrast to God's new order. (See Gal 1:4; 1 Cor 7:31.) The relativism of cultural practice is to be forsaken in favor of God's transforming and absolute truth.

Getty Images

The phrase "be transformed by the renewing of your mind" (v. 2) conveys the picture of metamorphosis. Indeed, the word "transformed" in the Greek denotes a metamorphosis from one form of life to another. The idea is graphically illustrated by the change of a tadpole into a frog or a caterpillar into a butterfly. This transformation of our minds from

A CLOSER LOOK

"Spiritual worship"

The expression "spiritual worship" found in Romans 12:1 comes from two Greek words *logiken latreian* that refer to the practice of serving and honoring a superior. The word *logiken* sounds like the word logical and denotes a reasonable reverence. The word *latreian* carries the idea of ministry and honor to God. Consequently the phrase "spiritual worship" can be translated as "reasonable service" (KJV) or "spiritual service of worship" (NASB).

foolish thinking toward godly wisdom does not happen by our own effort. No amount of infected rationalism can result in righteous intelligence. When we obey God's command and submit our minds to His spirit in obedience to His Word, we "discern what is the good, pleasing, and perfect will of God."

Do God's Will in the Church
(Rom. 12:3-8)

God created His church as an organism instead of an organization. He established it as a living, breathing body with many parts to accomplish His will. Consequently, believers from all walks of life, bearing unique personalities and marked by different races, are expected to fulfill God's will in fellowship with one another. Doing God's will in community with other believers starts with a correct assessment of ourselves and an honest appraisal of our spiritual gifts.

We damage the health of our churches when we either overrate or underestimate ourselves. Sometimes we minimize the abilities God gives us, but more often we overestimate our importance in the church. For this reason we are challenged to "think sensibly" (v. 3) and develop an accurate perspective of our role in the family of faith. For people who owe everything to God's grace, there is no room for pathetic inferiority on the one hand or pompous elitism on the other.

LEARNING ACTIVITY

Just Do It!

Respect God's will by identifying one aspect of your life in which you will begin to do God's will in at least one of the following areas. Write a specific commitment that reflects you're not only discerning, but doing God's will.

In the church (Rom. 12:3-8)

Through love (Rom. 12:9-21)

As a neighbor (Rom. 13:1-14)

Consider enlisting a prayer partner, asking him or her to hold you accountable for how you plan to follow God's will.

Notice that Paul emphasized both divine sovereignty and gift diversity. God distributes His gifts to us according to His sovereign purpose. The gifts, however, function differently as indicated by the phrase "all the parts do not have the same function" (v. 4). The diversity of gifts is not haphazard or random, but intentional so that all believers might fulfill God's will. Paul referred to the human body as an illustration of unity in diversity. The reference to "one body" (vv. 4-5) indicates the interrelated connection of believers exercising their spiritual gifts. Diversity without unity leads to division. Unity without diversity leads to stagnant uniformity.

Paul enumerated seven spiritual gifts. The gifts are not exhaustive, but illustrative of their value in the church body. (See 1 Cor. 12:8-10.)

Prophecy. The gift of prophecy refers to the practice of proclaiming the truth of God. It is more prescriptive than predictive.

Service. The word "service" in the Greek is the same word from which we derive the word "deacon." The spiritual gift of service touches everyone in the church. The practical ministry of greeting, ushering, carrying for preschoolers, serving on the audio-visual team, or driving the disabled and disadvantaged to the doctor's office or the grocery store is invaluable in the body.

Teaching. The gift of teaching involves both the content of information and the act of conveying the information. My daughter, Heather, is a mother of three children and she is beautifully gifted as a teacher. My son, Wes, serves the Lord in ministry and he, too, is dynamically gifted to communicate truth in a way that invites acceptance. How do you know if you have this gift? You will have a burning desire to impart truth into other's lives, but you will be gifted by God to do it in a way that enhances personal and spiritual growth in others.

Exhortation. The gift of exhortation is sometimes translated as "encouragement." The core meaning of exhortation involves the practice of stimulating, motivating, and admonishing others for the good of the body and for the glory of God.

Giving. Individuals with the gift of giving are instructed to practice it "with generosity" (v. 8). Givers carry blessings to the body and the exercise of their gift should never be for self-importance or self-promotion. To give generously is to give with the single-minded purpose of gratitude and big-hearted humility.

Leadership. The gift of leadership is crucial to the body of Christ and it must be practiced "with diligence" (v. 8c). The basic meaning of diligence denotes carefulness. Individuals with this gift should be careful to use it in a way that fortifies the health of the church and expands the ministry of the church.

Mercy. I love being around believers who have the gift of mercy. Whenever mercy is showered on the sick and suffering it acts as a healing ointment. Believers who possess the gift of mercy are cautioned to maintain "cheerfulness" (v. 8d) so that the recipients of mercy won't feel inferior or subordinate.

For Your Consideration

Can you identify the members of your church who have these gifts?

Prophecy: _____

Service: _____

Teaching: _____

Exhortation: _____

Giving: _____

Leadership: _____

Mercy: _____

Do God's Will Through Love
(Rom. 12:9-21)

Love is the foremost virtue of a believer. Having been justified by faith and endowed with spiritual gifts, a believer is under orders to practice love. Jesus made it clear that the way people will know we are His followers is by love. (See John 13:35.)

Paul specifically emphasized the imperative of love toward two broad groups: (1) the family of faith and (2) the alliance of antagonists. The practice of love is not an anemic sentimental emotion; it is an authentic and robust activity. The Greek word for love is the word *agape* and can never be linked to "hypocrisy" (v. 9). It is genuine to the core and self-sacrificing. It is a holy, saturated love that abhors "evil."

Paul pointed out that such love does not indulge in evil. Since *agape* love is from God, and God is opposed to evil, a believer who longs to fulfill the will of God makes every effort to steer clear of evil. Doing God's will in His church is always advanced by love between believers.

Notice how Paul stacked imperative upon imperative. For example, believers are directed to "show family affection" and "outdo one another in showing honor" (v. 10). By the authority of God's Word, believers are charged to demonstrate respect and loving preference for one another.

In a culture where everyone wants to be number one, believers should strive to be first: first to smile; first to delight in honoring others; first in "diligence" (v. 11); first in serving the Lord with enthusiasm; first to "rejoice in hope" (v. 12); first in patience when hard times strike; first to persist in "prayer"; and first to "pursue hospitality" (v. 13). The world would turn its attention toward Christ if more of us who call ourselves Christians would simply do God's will in relating to one another.

Doing God's will is not limited to our actions toward other believers. We also demonstrate God's will when we respond with love toward antagonists and critics of Christianity. The clear instruction calls for us to "bless" and "not curse" those who persecute us (v. 14). Such a response of non-retaliation requires absolute reliance on God's purpose. When personal hurts are answered by vengeful deeds, the will of God is not advanced. Instead of retaliation toward antagonists, believers should practice evangelization by relating to the common human experiences of rejoicing and weeping (v. 15). Everyone likes to be complimented when life is joyful and everyone likes to be comforted when life is hard.

Paul reinforced the theme of relating to antagonists and added the caveat, "If possible … live at peace with everyone" (v. 18) and "Do not be conquered by evil, but conquer evil with good" (v. 21). We exhibit love and do God's will when we make every effort to establish harmony toward unbelievers and when we refuse to engage in vengeance. Evil cannot thrive in an atmosphere of contagious love and holiness.

Do God's Will as a Neighbor (Rom. 13:1-14)

Fulfilling God's will as a neighbor involves living as a good citizen and practicing compassionate behavior. Believers are citizens of human government and citizens of God's kingdom.

For Your Consideration
Try to imagine how you would react if you lived under a government that hindered your faith. How would you maintain a balance between obeying the government and obeying God?

Despite political corruption and governmental greed, we must recognize that God has ordained civil government. Paul explained that "everyone must submit to the governing authorities" (v. 1). This is not blind complicity to the state, but a clarion call to support and obey those in authority. Ultimately, all authority must bow before God.

Are there times when a believer may resist authority? Yes, but only when a believer is ordered to violate a clear command from God. Do you recall in Acts 4:19-20 when Peter and John were ordered not to preach or teach about Jesus? Their response indicated respect and submission to the civil authorities. They acknowledge the right of the Sanhedrin to "decide" and render a verdict, but they also appealed to the higher authority of God's will.

There are two main reasons believers are instructed to "submit" (vv. 1,5). The first is because the government is appointed by God to maintain stability and lawfulness by means of exact punishment upon anyone "who does wrong" (v. 4). A second reason believers are instructed to submit is "because of your conscience" (v. 5). Doing God's will as neighbor means exercising a godly conscience with respect toward authorities and laws. As believers we live by a higher standard not simply because of fear of punishment for violating civil law, but primarily because our conscience convicts us to do so in honor of God.

Notice Paul's summary statement: "Pay your obligations to everyone: taxes to those you owe taxes, tolls to those you owe tolls, respect to those you owe respect, and honor to those you owe honor" (v. 7). First-century believers in Rome recoiled with disgust over the imposition of taxes. Taxation was a volatile issue in that day, as it can be today. We may detest the immorality of persons holding political office and deplore their deceitful politics, but that does not allow us the privilege of disrespecting the office itself.

In addition Paul said, "Do not owe anyone anything, except to love one another" (v. 8). This statement has been interpreted as forbidding financial debt of any kind, but it is wiser to understand it in the context of our indebtedness to God's love. The emphasis falls more on devotion than debt. Indeed, believers must fulfill God's will as neighbors who promptly pay their bills and notes. But there is a debt that can never be paid off—the debt to "love your neighbor as yourself" (v. 9). The ledger of love for others can never be completed and closed.

Doing God's will as a neighbor is especially urgent because the end of the age is drawing nearer. It is time to "wake up from sleep" (v. 11)! A holy reveille has sounded for God's people to pursue His will by discarding "the deeds of darkness" and applying the "armor of light" (v. 12).

Furthermore, Paul warned that we should "make no plans to satisfy the fleshly desires" (v. 14). The will of God allows no place for the gratification of sinful appetites to the detriment of God's transforming purpose. When we stop circling the parking lot of life and enter the door of God's will, our consuming desire becomes pleasing Him instead of satisfying our flesh.

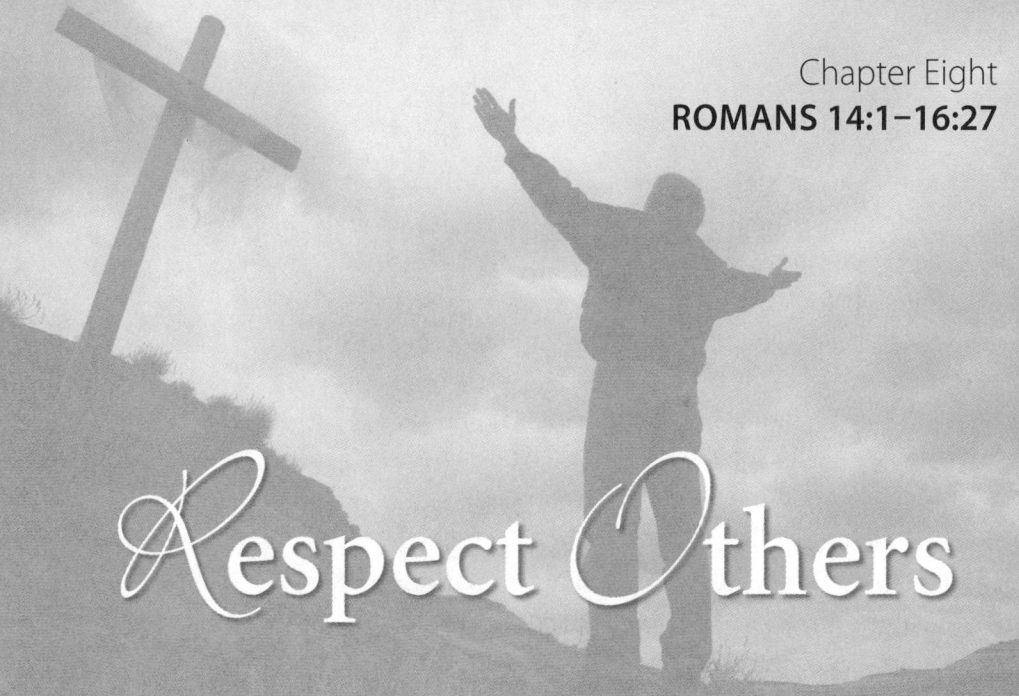

Respect Others

BIBLE TRUTH:
Believers are to respect others, which includes saying and doing only what has a positive impact on them.

LIFE IMPACT:
To help you show you respect other people

Do Not Criticize Others (Rom. 14:1-12)

My friend Tom, whom you met in the first chapter, walks courageously with Christ today. We stay in touch across the miles and recall mutual adventures in the faith many winters ago. He is my brother in the Lord, but we hold different opinions on some practical issues related to Christian living. I hold strong convictions about some implications drawn from God's Word that he hasn't embraced. Nevertheless, our common reverence for the inerrancy of Scripture and our shared passion for Jesus compel us toward a deep and affectionate respect for one another.

The call for believers to show their respect for one another is not a call to ignore obvious differences or to water down clear instruction from God. It is not an appeal to minimize essential biblical doctrines regarding man's depravity, God's grace, justifica-

LEARNING ACTIVITY

R-E-S-P-E-C-T

Use the letters below to help you think of specific ways you can show your respect for others. Notice you may use letters anywhere in the words or phrases you list.

_____ R _____

_____ E _____

_____ S _____

_____ P _____

_____ E _____

_____ C _____

_____ T _____

tion by faith, Jesus' atonement, His resurrection, or His second coming.

The plea for acceptance and respect consistently occurs within the context of believers' need to live in community with others so Christ may be glorified. The word "accept" (v. 1) means "receive" or "welcome" and carries the idea of full inclusion into a fellowship. But what does it mean to "accept anyone who is weak in faith"?

The answer is found within the cultural background and theological context of the congregation at Rome. Two broad groups consisting of Gentiles and Jews were struggling to apply the gospel in light of their respective customs and traditions. Paul referred to those who felt constrained to keep the dietary customs of Jewish heritage as the "weak" (14:1). Those who felt liberated from such rules and regulations Paul called the "strong" (15:1). Consequently, the command to "accept anyone who is weak in faith" served as an imperative for strong believers to resist criticizing individuals whose conscience was still influenced by old customs. The prohibition "don't argue about doubtful issues" (v. 1) may be paraphrased as "don't be contentious about matters of secondary importance." The primary issue is harmony between believers so that the weak in faith experience the embrace of fellowship from the strong in faith. Neither strong nor weak believers should hold contempt for what others eat or don't eat.

Paul not only addressed the tension regarding the dietary restrictions, he also addressed the conflict regarding sacred days. Obviously, the Sabbath held special reverence for the Jews as did selective feasts days. But for others, especially Gentile Christians, the first day of the week was set aside as a day of worship, and Jewish feast days were regarded as no different than ordinary days. What did Paul offer as a solution? Paul explained that each believer "must be fully convinced in his own mind" (v. 5). In other words, as a believer I am cautioned not to violate my conscience in conformity to the conscience of another believer. On the other hand, I must not persuade another believer to violate his or her conscience to conform to my conscience.

Furthermore, all believers—strong and weak—must practice mutual submission to Christ. The acknowledgement and application of Christ's lordship is crucial to the harmony of a community of believers. Consequently, the statement "whether we live or die, we belong to the Lord" (v. 8) emphasizes His authority in personal relationships. The purpose of His death and resurrection was to verify His "rule over both the dead and the living" (v. 9). The word "rule" comes from a Greek verb that denotes mastery and ownership. We are not at liberty to insist on our own way when it is contrary to Christ's instruction. Because Jesus is Lord we are answerable to Him for our attitudes and actions toward others. Regrettably, contentious and critical behavior among believers seriously hinders the mission of the church and slanders the authority of Christ.

The decisive reason for withholding criticism of one another is because the right to judge belongs to Him. The statement "we will all stand before the judgment seat of God" (v. 10) reinforces the truth that condescension and criticism of others will not elevate our status one bit when we stand before the all-knowing Lord. We should relate to others with the serious reminder that one day "each of us will give an account of himself to God" (v. 12). There is no neutrality regarding this fact. The term "each" involves every person. The term "us" is personally inclusive so that we cannot apply it to other believers without applying it to ourselves. The term "account" denotes the keeping of a record. God keeps a complete and perfect record of every motive, decision, and deed. Unlike our inaccurate judgments and uninformed accusations, God renders a flawless assessment of every individual.

For Your Consideration

What actions are necessary for conflict resolution between believers today?

Do What Encourages Others
(Rom. 14:13-23)

The practice of encouragement is one of the best ways to show respect to others. Instead of tearing down others by criticism, Paul advocated building up others by encouragement. Think about it. Don't you enjoy the fellowship of an encourager?

Paul established the case for respect through encouragement by three relationship principles. First, we should not allow our liberty to cause other believers to stumble. The statement "decide not to put a stumbling block or pitfall in your brother's way" (v. 13) is an emphatic call for action. A "stumbling block" refers to anything carelessly unattended that causes another believer to stumble. A "pitfall" refers to anything that deliberately ensnares a person in a trap. Believers can set an encouraging example by avoiding activities that lead others into sin. Paul explained that although "nothing is unclean in itself" (v. 14), if participation in it tempts a weak believer to violate his conscience, then a strong believer should practice restraint.

Second, we can pursue mutual edification. Paul plainly advocated the pursuit of peace that "builds up one another" (v. 19). The work of God suffers incalculable damage when believers are more interested in the pursuit of their preference than in the practice of their love. Carefully consider the exhortation "do not tear down God's work because of food" (v. 20).

For Your Consideration

1. Instead of food, what practices stir strife between contemporary believers?

2. In what ways do church members tear down God's work?

Perhaps the food battle of the first-century church resembles some worship battles of the twenty-first century church. Resolution and reconciliation occur when believers agree that the styles of worship are secondary to the Savior we worship. Within the boundary of absolute truth and redeeming love there are widely divergent styles that honor Christ. Consequently, before a believer acts on a strongly held opinion, he must consider how an action will affect the work of God and the edification of other believers. The spiritual growth of others and the advancement of God's kingdom must always be an application consistently practiced in the church.

A third relationship principle involves the regulation and responsibility of our faith in a community of believers. Notice the beatitude "blessed is the man who does not condemn himself by what he approves" (v. 22). Indeed we have liberty in our faith, but not liberty to flaunt our faith as superior to other believers. With every blessed freedom God grants to a believer, there is a corresponding responsibility to exercise that freedom in a manner that God approves. God never rewards any activity on behalf of a believer that harms the faith of another believer. I must exercise caution so that what I approve lines up with what God approves.

The concluding phrase, "everything that is not from faith is sin" (v. 23), transcends the situation facing the believers at Rome. It is a principle reflective of Paul's entire presentation of the gospel. Faith as reliance on God is fundamental to salvation and sanctification. Life in Christ is impossible without faith and life among believers is imperfect without it. Furthermore, this phrase summarizes Paul's plea for respect through encouragement. God bids us to walk in faith and to steer clear of the "gray areas," as we sometimes call the practices that fall between the colors of certainty. Perhaps you heard from a parent the same home-spun wisdom my mother often whispered to me, "Stay away from gray—it can lead to grime."

Do What Pleases Others (Rom. 15:1-7)

The Lord is deeply concerned about the unity of believers and frequently referred to its importance. In His intercessory prayer recorded in John 17, Jesus asked the Father to keep believers unified in a oneness like that shared by God the Father and God the Son. Similarly, Paul applied his Savior's desire for unity in his instruction to the believers at Rome. Paul mentioned four reasons why we should strive to please one another.

The first reason is because pleasing others can enhance their spiritual maturity. The responsibility of respecting and pleasing one another applies to all believers, but special emphasis falls upon those who are strong. Stronger believers have "an obligation to bear the weaknesses of those without strength, and not to please ourselves" (v. 1). The word "bear" denotes the carrying of a burden and the endurance of problems. You may realize that a weaker believer faces many problems brought upon his life through unfortunate circumstances or unwise choices. To "bear" with him means more than token tolerance of his problems. It means that you, as a stronger believer, must carry the burden with him by showing respect and practical sensitivity. The qualifying phrases "for his good" and "in order to build him up" (v. 2) specify the reason for pleasing others. By no stretch of interpretation should the idea of pleasing others include the practice of immoral activity. The meaning of "for his good" refers to his spiritual maturity and growth in Christ. The purpose of building him up requires the sacrifice of our time, energy, and personal choices in order to equip him.

A second reason for pleasing others centers on the example Jesus set for us. Jesus didn't come to earth to die on the cross because he looked forward to the excruciating pain of crucifixion. Despite His sinless life, Jesus took our sin because of an unflinching commitment to please the Father. The fact that "the Messiah did not please Himself" captures the essence of His life and work. Paul quoted from Psalm 69:9 to reinforce this point. The "insults" (v. 3), or reproaches, declare that in pleasing the Father he suffered for us and vicariously atoned for our sin.

A CLOSER LOOK

Hospitality

When Paul commended Phoebe (16:1) to the believers at Rome, he was requesting hospitality on her behalf. Hospitality played a significant role in domestic life across the Roman Empire and especially in Paul's missionary travels. Although ancient inns or hotels existed, many were unsuitable and posed as havens for criminals and prostitutes. The best place to stay was in the home of a friend or in the home of a stranger known to practice hospitality to guests. It was common for people to write letters recommending an individual who was traveling to a place where other friends lived. Paul appealed to the believers at Rome to embrace Phoebe as a sister in Christ, to extend a loving welcome and thereby demonstrate the practice of hospitality. (See 12:13.)

If our Lord Jesus Christ did not pursue personal advantage to please himself, shouldn't we set aside our selfish privileges for His sake and for the sake of His church?

For Your Consideration
1. What implications does this truth hold for the community of believers where you serve?

2. What practical examples could you flesh out that would demonstrate how your love for Jesus pleases His church?

A third reason to please others comes from the instruction provided by Scripture. Notice the striking relevance of Scripture. Everything written in Scripture is relevant and applicable today because it speaks to our deepest needs. Three words demand our attention regarding the role of Scripture in pleasing others: "endurance," "encouragement," and "hope" (v. 4). So often when a body of believers face a difficulty, the Word of God whispers for them to persevere through the trial. How many times has Scripture brought encouraging showers to the parched soil of your soul? Because of the written Word, we know the "hope" of eternal life through God's living Word, His Son, our Savior. Therefore we endure differences, encourage maturity, and labor with the hope for the unity of believers here on earth that we will share one day in heaven.

A fourth and final reason for pleasing others is for the sake of God's glory. Linger on the summary purpose phrase: "so that you may glorify the God and Father of our Lord Jesus Christ with a united mind and voice" (v. 6). The ultimate purpose of unity focuses on God's glory and on pleasing Him. The primary question that every believer should ask is this: How am I glorifying the Lord in my relationships with others? The phrase "with a united mind and voice" is a unity that falls at the feet of the crucified Savior. The ship of fellowship sinks unless we are unified for His glory.

Essentially, church life is not about me or you, although we are obviously involved. It is not primarily about policy, programs, or personalities, although those factors do count. First and foremost a church is designed to be a body of believers passionately in love with Jesus, pursuing His mission by His Spirit, and all together for His glory.

Biblical Illustrator

Cenchreae, the main seaport for Corinth. Phoebe was a member of the church in Cenchreae (16:1) and likely delivered Paul's letter to the Romans.

Do What Commends Others
(Rom. 16:1-4)

Believers who show respect toward one another are not reluctant to practice commendation. Consequently, Paul wrote to the believers at Rome saying, "I commend to you our sister Phoebe" (v. 1). Letters of commendation were common throughout the Roman Empire. Since Phoebe was the person entrusted with the task of carrying the epistle to the Romans, Paul wanted to make sure she was warmly received. He gave specific instruction for the congregation to welcome her in a "manner worthy of the saints" (v. 2). In other words, Paul was asking the believers to open widely their hearts and homes as a testimony of hospitality. Obviously, the believers needed to know something about Phoebe, so

LEARNING ACTIVITY

One

Because the Lord is deeply concerned about the unity of believers, He frequently referred to its importance. In His intercessory prayer recorded in John 17, Jesus asked the Father to keep believers unified in a oneness like that shared by God the Father and God the Son. Similarly, Paul applied his Savior's desire for unity in his instruction to the believers at Rome. (See Rom. 15:1-7.) Underline the occurrences of the word "one" throughout John 17. Read the verses aloud, pausing after each sentence to reflect for a few moments. Consider writing a prayer asking God to help you be "one" as Jesus prayed.

Paul explained that she was "a servant of the church in Cenchreae." The word "servant" in this context does not refer to a specific office in the church, but a general practice of ministry. Servant is a term used to describe all followers of Christ. There is no evidence that Paul used "servant" to refer to a church office such as deacon, particularly at this early stage of Christianity.

Phoebe's hometown of Cenchreae was located five miles east of Corinth on the Saronic Gulf and it served as the main seaport for Corinth. Perhaps Phoebe had been converted as a result of Paul's preaching and ministry at Corinth, or she may have heard the gospel and followed Christ through the witness of another believer in Cenchreae. Regardless, Paul commended her to the congregation at Rome as "a benefactor of many—and of me also" (v. 2). The term "benefactor" comes from a Greek word that denotes a person of influence and prominence. Phoebe was probably a woman who used her influence and wealth to help the believers in Cenchreae as well as Paul in his missionary journeys.

In addition to Phoebe, Paul commended or greeted 26 other individuals as he concluded his letter to the Romans. He gave special attention to Prisca and Aquila, "who risked their own necks for my life" (v. 4). "Prisca" is a shortened form of Priscilla, the wife of Aquila (Acts 18:2). Together they labored alongside of Paul to advance the gospel at Corinth and at Rome.

For Your Consideration

1. If you were making a list of individuals who sacrificially serve Christ in your church, who would you include?

_____

_____

2. As you reflect on your journey with Christ, to what persons do you need to write a letter of respect or commendation?

_____

_____

3. How have you risked your neck for the sake of the gospel?

_____

_____

Please join me in a fervent prayer that our Lord Jesus Christ would enable us to spread the gospel as contagiously in our generation as Paul did in his generation!

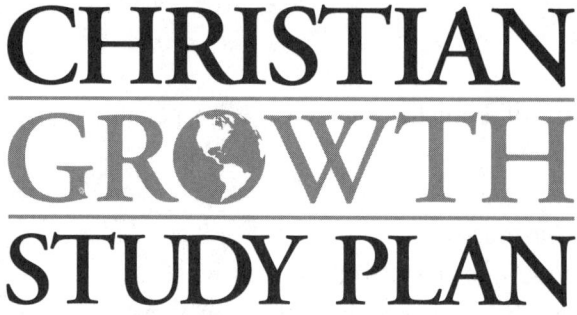

CHRISTIAN GROWTH STUDY PLAN

In the **Christian Growth Study Plan (formerly Church Study Course),** this book, *God's Amazing Grace: Studies in Romans,* is a resource for course credit in the subject area Leadership and Skill Development of the Christian Growth category of plans. To receive credit, read the book, complete the learning activities, show your work to your pastor, a staff member, or church leader, then complete the following information. This page may be duplicated. Send the completed page to:

Christian Growth Study Plan • One LifeWay Plaza • Nashville, TN 37234-0117 • FAX: (615) 251-5067 • **Email:** *cgspnet@lifeway.com.*

For information about the Christian Growth Study Plan, refer to the Christian Growth Study Plan Catalog. It is located online at *www.lifeway.com/cgsp.* If you do not have access to the Internet, contact the Christian Growth Study Plan office at (800) 968-5519 for the specific plan you need for your ministry.

God's Amazing Grace: Studies in Romans
COURSE NUMBER: **CG-1176**

PARTICIPANT INFORMATION

Social Security Number (USA ONLY-optional) | Personal CGSP Number* | Date of Birth (MONTH, DAY, YEAR)

Name (First, Middle, Last) | Home Phone

Address (Street, Route, or P.O. Box) | City, State, or Province | Zip/Postal Code

Email Address for CGSP use

Please check appropriate box: ❑ Resource purchased by church ❑ Resource purchased by self ❑ Other

CHURCH INFORMATION

Church Name

Address (Street, Route, or P.O. Box) | City, State, or Province | Zip/Postal Code

CHANGE REQUEST ONLY

☐ Former Name

☐ Former Address | City, State, or Province | Zip/Postal Code

☐ Former Church | City, State, or Province | Zip/Postal Code

Signature of Pastor, Conference Leader, or Other Church Leader | Date

*New participants are requested but not required to give SS# and date of birth. Existing participants, please give CGSP# when using SS# for the first time. Thereafter, only one ID# is required. **Mail to:** Christian Growth Study Plan, One LifeWay Plaza, Nashville, TN 37234-0117. Fax: (615)251-5067.

Revised 4-05